T0328758

GARLAND STUDIES ON

# INDUSTRIAL PRODUCTIVITY

*edited by*
STUART BRUCHEY
ALLAN NEVINS PROFESSOR EMERITUS
COLUMBIA UNIVERSITY

# THE IMPACT OF INFORMATION TECHNOLOGY

## EVIDENCE FROM THE HEALTHCARE INDUSTRY

NIRUP M. MENON

Routledge
Taylor & Francis Group

LONDON AND NEW YORK

First published 2000 by Garland Publishing, Inc.

Published 2020 by Routledge
2 Park Square, Milton Park, Abingdon, Oxon OX14 4RN
605 Third Avenue, New York, NY 10017

First issued in paperback 2021

*Routledge is an imprint of the Taylor & Francis Group, an informa business*

Publisher's Note
The publisher has gone to great lengths to ensure the quality of this reprint but points out that some imperfections in the original copies may be apparent.

**Library of Congress Cataloging-in-Publication Data**
Library of Congress Cataloging-in-Publication Data is available
from the Library of Congress.

The impact of information technology : evidence from the healthcare industry / by Nirup M. Menon

ISBN 13: 978-1-138-99791-2 (pbk)
ISBN 13: 978-0-8153-3447-7 (hbk)
ISBN 13: 978-0-203-82073-5 (ebk)

DOI: 10.4324/9780203820735

# Acknowledgments

I owe a lifetime of gratitude to Dr. Byungtae Lee, the chairperson of my dissertation committee, and a mentor and friend, who has taken me as his "apprentice" in order to educate and train me for a life of research and teaching. He has taught me many new and interesting ways of looking at research challenges in the field of information technology. I am very grateful to Dr. Leslie Eldenburg for providing me guidance in the health economics area and for unhesitatingly providing me the data for the research without which the dissertation would have remained just a theoretical exercise. I am indebted to Dr. Sudha Ram, Dr. David Pingry, and Dr. Edward Zajac, members of the committee, from whom I received full support during the course of the program.

The financial support, the computer support and the secretarial support from the Department of MIS at the University of Arizona is gratefully acknowledged.

Finally and most importantly, I am eternally indebted to my parents, Col. (Dr.) M.S. Menon and Mrs. Jayasree Menon for taking complete interest in and for paying undivided attention to my education during my formative years at school.

# Contents

# List of Figures

# List of Tables

# Preface

This book is a revised edition of a doctoral dissertation submitted to the faculty of the University of Arizona. When I began the dissertation work in 1995, the Internet and the World Wide Web were just gaining public attention. Companies were beginning to spend more on information technology (IT) than ever before. Given the rapid development in IT in the past decades, the equally rapid adoption of these technologies by companies, and the ongoing debate on the value of IT, I believed that a study on the impact of IT of firms could be interesting and useful. The techniques presented in this book complement existing research on IT impacts. These techniques can also be adapted and extended to measure more precisely the returns from hardware, software, and other capitol investments.

Theoretical and empirical analyses are reported in order to explain the productivity "paradox" surrounding IT. The techniques used in the study cover a wide range from simple deterministic production functions to panel data techniques and data envelopment analysis. The empirical study is set in the health care industry. A hospital, which is the unit of analysis, is an organizational entity that provides an appropriate context for the study of the interactions between information technology, technological advancements, organizational factors, and regulation. Overall, it was found that IT contributes in a positive manner to the production of healthcare services. However, measurement problems including "quality" of IT capital due to technological developments can lead to the underestimation of IT productivity. It is also seen that regulation plays a major role in the manner in which costs are allocated to input factors. In particular, the effect of the Prospective Payment System (PPS) legislated in 1983 is investigated. One of the findings of the cost function analysis is that, since PPS, hospitals have been moving toward cost containment. Nonparametric analyses is used to determine the allocative inefficiency in IT with respect to other inputs. The different techniques serve as means to triangulate the measure of IT impact on productivity and efficiency, and in addition, develop the theory underlying production techniques.

# CHAPTER 1

# Introduction

Information technology (IT) has become important to the very survival of organizations. Information technology spending in the U.S. has increased from a few million dollars in 1970 to over $50 billion in 1990 (Jorgenson and Stiroh, 1995). Industry analysts and economists have observed a "co-incidental" slowdown in the productivity of the U.S. economy during the same period (e.g., Bell et al., 1991). While it is possible that the slowdown may have been caused by a variety of reasons other than IT-related phenomena, the possibility that IT may be one of reasons for this slowdown has led researchers to attempt to extract a measure of the value of IT in the production of goods and services (Brynjolofsson and Hitt, 1994). It has been suggested that the slowdown in the productivity of the economy is a contrivance of the techniques used for observation, measurement, and analysis and that it is not a real phenomenon in itself (Romer, 1987). Studies also showed that investments in IT may have been misspent. These studies do so by showing that the productivity contribution of IT was empirically shown to be negative (e.g., Roach, 1987). Other explanations of the IT effect on general productivity include the finding that IT creates surplus for consumers but not for producers, thereby diluting the productivity contribution of IT (Breshnahan, 1986; Brynjolofsson and Hitt, 1996). These latter studies have added much to the understanding of the business value of IT.

In understanding the impact of IT on the economy, history lends insight when we compare the technological revolution of computers and information systems with the technological revolution that stemmed from innovations such as steam engines (Simon, 1986) or the dynamo

(David, 1990). The instantaneous productivity improvements that were expected from the steam engine and the dynamo were not observed partly because of the need to re-organize the production operations. Introduction of IT has led to similar attempts of reorganization (Hammer and Champy, 1992). The two factors—(1) the need for observing the changes in the use of new technology over time and (2) the complexity of analytical treatment of IT impact on firms—lead to the conclusion that the effect of IT on the productivity of the firm, industry, and economy is best judged using longitudinal, empirical studies.

In general, productivity growth and the contribution of inputs to productivity growth has been empirically measured using index numbers (Harris and Katz, 1991) or econometric techniques (Schmidt and Lovell, 1979; Kumbhakar, 1990). Among the several major differences between the two techniques, the index numbers technique assumes away inefficiency in production which econometric techniques are capable of modeling, whereas econometric techniques make several assumptions to simplify computation and are subject to specification error. Since productivity and efficiency are inextricably linked, the productivity approach is a more appropriate technique than the index number approach for modeling inefficiency of production that results from bounded rationality, regulation and labor unionization. Managerial inefficiency can take two forms—technical inefficiency that results from the inability of the production process to produce the maximum output for a level of inputs used (due to poor engineering design, regulation, etc.) and allocative inefficiency that results from selecting a technically efficient input mix that is not optimal in cost (due to labor unionization, the inability to observe prices of inputs, etc.).

Productivity analysis of IT can be conducted at an economy, industry, firm or process level. While economy- and industry-level analyses may confound results due to aggregation of data and heterogeneity of units of analysis, process-level analyses may suffer from other equally serious problems such as insufficient sample size and the validity in the generalization of results. Since IT productivity in a firm cannot be determined in isolation but has to be determined in relation to other factors such as human resource strategy and external economic institutions (Osterman 1990), a multifactor, firm-level productivity analysis seems to be the most appropriate line of inquiry. In a firm-level analysis, a sample of homogeneous firms should be chosen to minimize confounding from other factors when eliciting productivity contribution of IT. For example, the firms should belong to one industry.

One way to empirically elicit productivity contribution of inputs is to assume a functional form for the technology that transforms inputs into outputs. The second way is to compare the amounts of input used and outputs produced for each firm relative to other firms in the sample without specifying a functional form for the production technology. The former technique is called the parametric technique and the latter is called the nonparametric technique. In this study, the productivity of various input factors and the various efficiencies are determined by both parametric and nonparametric techniques. The results from the various models from both techniques are triangulated, and the interplay between the efficiencies and the organization's environment is also studied.

The setting for the study is the healthcare industry. This industry makes an interesting arena because of the recent increase in hospital IT spending and cost-cutting initiatives in the industry. The healthcare industry is a highly regulated industry which allows the studying of regulation effects on investment patterns with possible insight for policymakers. Because the industry is heavily regulated, hospitals collect and maintain data on spending and earnings. This data is very suitable for a firm-level study. The organizational choices of hospitals, such as teaching status, also provide a context for studying the relation between organizational choice and IT productivity.

This book is organized as follows. In Chapter 2, I review literature pertinent to IT impact issues discussed above and in the rest of the book. In Chapter 3, I review the history and background of the healthcare industry. The field data used in the analysis is explained in Chapter 4. Chapter 5 contains the production function approach to studying IT impact whereas Chapter 6 contains a cost function approach to studying the effect of regulation on capital investments including IT investments. Chapter 7 contains a nonparametric approach to IT productivity and efficiency studies in an effort to triangulate results from parametric techniques in Chapters 5 and 6. Chapter 8 contains a discussion of results and concludes the book with remarks on future research directions.

# CHAPTER 2

# Productivity Literature

## 2.1 BUSINESS VALUE OF IT

A manager of a management information systems (MIS) department in a firm is concerned with measuring the success of the department. He/she can evaluate a specific project's success or the department's success from various perspectives such as system quality, information quality, the rate of use of the system, user satisfaction, individual impact and organizational impact (DeLone and McLean 1992). The former five are considered internal to the firm in the sense that these are indicators of performance of intermediate business/social processes that lead to the realization of one or more final organizational goal(s). On the other hand, organizational impact is a direct indicator of the impact of IT on the realization of the final organization goal and subsumes the effects from the other five success measures. Organizational impact of IT indicates the impact of IT investments or usage in relation to the organization's external environment such as markets, consumers, competition, etc. Among the five perspectives listed above, organizational performance has been rated higher than the others by information systems (IS) practitioners as an indicator of IS performance (Brancheau and Wetherbe 1987). Organizational impact is a broad term that captures several dimensions of organizational performance. Three primary dimensions are productivity, profitability and consumer surplus (Brynjolfsson and Hitt 1996). In this study, I focus on the productivity dimension of IT as a measure of the business value of IT.

## 2.2 THE MODERN PRODUCTIVITY PARADOX

Before reviewing IT productivity literature, a foray into the modern productivity paradox literature is warranted. The paradox has come about as a result of the contradiction between the commonly held perception that technological innovations lead to higher productivity and the observed fact that the productivity of the advanced economies is slowing down (e.g., Bell et al., 1990). Since the initial discovery of this contradiction in the early 1980s, researchers and policymakers have devoted a large amount of time, several journal articles and seminars attempting to determine whether the contradiction is a statistical artifact or a real phenomenon. The unravelling of the paradox requires understanding the computer revolution and the impacts of IT in organizations.

David (1990, 1991) likens the computer revolution to the technological revolution fostered by the invention of the dynamo. He postulates that the postindustrial era can be divided into technoeconomic regimes punctuated by innovations in technology (David, 1991). He observes that analysts predicted dramatic changes in the technoeconomic system due to dynamos but failed to see the fruition of these changes due to the effort expended on the reorganization of factory plants and the work environment. He suggests that similarly the computer revolution will not directly and immediately translate into dramatic productivity improvements. The "slippage between advancing frontier of technology and actual practice" can only be overcome by significant reorganization and reconfiguration of productive activity over a period of time. The literature on business process re-engineering over the past decade is based on a similar vein of thought (e.g., Hammer and Champy, 1993).

Researchers have observed another surprising aspect during the productivity slow-down in economy. Since the late 1980s, the productivity of the manufacturing sector has been rising while the productivity growth of the service sector has become negative (Baily and Gordon, 1988). Adding to the conundrum is the fact that 80 or more percent of the capital in the service sector is IT capital. These observations and results intensify the debate on the impact of IT on firms. The following sections review the results of previous studies on IT productivity issues.

## 2.3 IT AND THE PRODUCTIVITY PARADOX

Since the inception of the use of IT in business, one primary area of IT application has been in transaction processing to speed up clerical work and to cut labor costs. That is, increasing productivity and reducing costs were primary reasons for using IT. However, until recently research has not shown that the use of IT leads to an increase in productivity. I believe that one of the problems is methodical in that most previous studies use a growth-accounting or an index numbers approach to determining productivity wherein inefficiency in production is not modeled (which is indeed difficult to do at an aggregate economy or industry level).

In a study involving the impacts of any input (such as IT), measuring the productivity (by how much the output of a firm, industry, or economy has changed by the use of the input) is a central issue. IT productivity analysis can be approached from various levels pertaining to the unit of analysis. There have been economy-, industry-, firm-, and process-level analyses that have studied the productivity impact of IT. Economy-level studies have primarily been reported in economics journals. The primary concern of many of these studies is to investigate the decline in the productivity of the service sector in the 1970s and 1980s and to determine the reasons for the decline despite increasing investments in IT capital.

### 2.3.1 IT and Economy-Level Productivity

As described above, researchers were intrigued by the stagnation in the productivity of the economy since the 1970s. In particular, the productivity growth of the service sector has been negative and this has been so despite the large investments by the service sector in IT capital. One of the key measures used to study productivity has been average labor productivity at the economy level. Change in the average labor productivity (ALP) is defined as the change in the output for a unit change in labor-hours and change in multifactor productivity (MFP) is defined as the change in the output for a unit change in labor-hours and capital weighted by their shares in total cost (Baily and Gordon, 1988, p. 356). The problem with the ALP measure is that the output–labor ratio does not capture important firm-level effects such as substitution/complementarities between different types of capital and between capital and labor. Similarly, MFP suffers from problems such as the assumption of constant returns to scale of production and equality of nominal income share for each input and its output elasticity. In addition, aggregation at the economy level requires use of "aggregate" price deflators which are of highly suspect derivation and meaning.

The growth accounting framework uses a similar formulation but differs in that it is defined in terms of rates of change for output and inputs (e.g., see Oliner and Sichel, 1994). The assumptions are similar to those described in the previous paragraph as are the pitfalls. Studies in economy-level productivity suggest that we use caution in the areas regarding (1) the specification of input and output, (2) the data collection including price and quality information of complex capital such as computer and communication equipment, (3) the measurement of aggregate capital data, (4) the methodologies used such as growth accounting and index numbers, etc. A comprehensive review of the various levels of studies in IT productivity and the approaches used therein is contained in Brynjolofsson and Yang (1996).

### 2.3.2 IT and Industry-Level Productivity

An industry-level study of productivity is useful, especially from the viewpoint of separating the manufacturing and service sectors, because the intensity and uses of IT investments and the productivity growth in the two sectors have not been very similar. Therefore, any errors introduced in economy-level studies by the aggregation of data from dissimilar sectors can be controlled for by industry-level analyses. Most studies in either sector, such as Berndt and Morrison (1995) or Siegel and Griliches (1992) in the manufacturing sector, or Roach (1991) in the service sector, have found no contribution from IT to industry-level productivity. However, industry-level studies, in spite of the separation into manufacturing and service sectors, also suffer from the same problems that have plagued economy-level studies. Indeed, just as in the physical sciences, reconciling observed microphenomena and observed macrophenomena is difficult in economics and in business also. Economy- and industry-level macromeasurements show productivity slowdown but the question is whether firm-level analysis will show similar results. A problem that arises is that macrodata does not capture or account for firm-level (micro) phenomena such as technical inefficiency, best-practice technology and differences in investment behavior among firms (Carlsson, 1990).

In both the economy-wide and industry-wide studies, typical methods of analysis are growth accounting (or index numbers) and regression analysis. Ratio analysis involves determining performance-to-investment ratios whereas regression analysis involves estimating the correlations between performance metrics and investments through linear regression models. Typically, at the economy and industry level, these models fail to explain much, other than providing evidence of correlation or no correlation (but not causality) between IT investment and performance. In addition, both the economy and industry level aggregation of data and measurement errors make interpretation of the results extremely difficult. Specifically, the implications with regard to decision making and policymaking will not be clear. And finally, these techniques assume away inefficiency in the amounts of input levels chosen by managers. Therefore, performance-to-investment ratios (or their average over a population) cannot be usefully interpreted.

On the other hand, more realistic models can be formulated in a firm-level analysis. Inefficiencies in resource allocation of inputs can be modeled and managerial behavior stemming from bounded rationality can be accounted for. After extracting away the inefficiency component, the input factor amounts will relate a more realistic account of their contribution to production. Baily and Gordon (1988) conclude that one of the explanations for the productivity paradox is that "computing equipment can be productive at the firm level and yet make little contribution to aggregate growth." In a firm-level analysis, it is possible to control for firm-specific and industry-specific aspects that might confound productivity studies. It is also particularly suited to studying substitution and complementarity effects between IT and other factors of production (Dewan and Min, 1996).

### 2.3.3 IT and Firm-Level Productivity

In the past, firm-level analyses have been conducted mainly in the manufacturing sector. Previous studies used ratio analysis, regression models based on growth-accounting models or a combination of both to study the effect of IT in one or more firms, in an Industry or in the economy. Ratio analysis and regression models may be the only possible method of analysis in industry- and economy-level studies because no additional information, economic or behavioral, is available for modeling an industry or the economy. These models are useful to study the correlation between IT investments and performance factors such as revenues, output amount, etc. However, no causality regarding productivity and IT investments at a firm-level can be determined nor can useful recommendations be made to decision-makers and practitioners regarding returns on IT investments. On the other hand, at the firm-level, additional information regarding managerial behavior can be added to a simple model in order to estimate richer and more reliable empirical models. The research in econometrics literature is based on this line of reasoning. In the long run, the competency of a firm in terms of product/service quality, strategic advantage, etc., achieved due to IT may translate into productivity increase and cost reduction. In this way, output and cost may very well capture other advantages of IT investments on firm performance. Following is a summary of firm-level analysis of IT impact on performance.

Following Hitt and Brynjolofsson (1996), organizational performance may be measured in terms of productivity, profitability and consumer surplus. While productivity and profitability measures account for the benefits accrued by the firm by using IT, consumer surplus measures the downstream benefits of product quality and market competition that consumers accrue due to the use of IT by producers (Bresnahan, 1986; Brynjolfsson, 1996).

Unfortunately, firm-level analyses have not been able to unravel much of the productivity paradox. The paradox remains because of the conflicting results from different studies. However, the studies have exposed the importance of the output/performance measures and the techniques used. The balance has tilted more in favor of positive IT contribution to productivity with a majority of recent studies finding that IT has a positive impact in terms productivity (Weill, 1992; Brynjolfsson and Hitt, 1996; Dewan and Min, 1996), profitability (Alpar and Kim 1991) or consumer surplus (Hitt and Brynjolfsson, 1996). Earlier, studies such as Strassman (1985, 1991) and Harris and Katz (1991) found weak or no correlation between IT ratios and financial performance ratios.

Most of the previous work cited above, excluding Brynjolofsson and Hitt (1996), suffer from the problem of using single-equation regression techniques. As explained in the subsequent chapters in this thesis, single-equation models can lead to inconsistent estimates of parameters and therefore, to wrong conclusions. A system of equations built upon robust microeconomic theory leads to consistent estimates (Greene, 1993) and, more important, leads to results that can be interpreted usefully. One other serious problem is the use of dollar amounts for capital rather than physical units. Production functions are specified in quantity space. If dollar amounts are used, then price of the inputs should be used to determine physical quantities of capital. Prices of capital are very difficult to obtain. This study shows how to avoid the above problems and how to estimate productivity of IT at a firm level using state-of-the-art econometric techniques.

## 2.3.4 IT and Process-Level Productivity

The process is a smaller unit of analysis than the firm. Using process-level analysis in IT impact studies can be useful because IT implementation affects processes before they affect the firms using those processes.

In IT literature, there has been only one process-level study of productivity. This paucity of research using the process as the unit of analysis may be a result of the difficulty in data collection such as finding sufficient number of similar processes across firms, separating IT effects from non-IT effects within a process and generalization problems arising from the difficulty of finding similar processes performed with and without IT across firms. Kelley (1994) looks at the effect of programmable automation used in manufacturing operations for several firms and finds that, on average, automation improves efficiency of processes and that firms have varying levels of success with IT. The results of Kelley (1994) lead us to believe that productivity and efficiency are intricately linked and any reasonable study of IT productivity must model inefficiencies of operation and management.

## 2.4 PRODUCTIVITY MEASUREMENT TECHNIQUES

Productivity measurement of firms, in addition to the above techniques such as growth accounting and ratio analysis, can be measured using parametric or nonparametric techniques. Parametric techniques are comprised of deterministic and stochastic approaches. While deterministic approaches implicitly assume that all firms use capital assets at the same level of efficiency, stochastic approaches assume that all production processes are inherently inefficient and model inefficiencies into the production process for each firm (Lovell, 1992). In addition to inefficient production process, all firms will implement technologies (or input factors) such as IT at varying levels of efficiency. For example, consider the case of IT capital where it is well known that IT "conversion effectiveness" is a determinant in the process of how IT creates business value (Weill, 1992). This is considered a more realistic picture of productivity and may lead to more reliable measures of the impact of input factors in productivity.

Parametric techniques assume a functional relationship between inputs and outputs. Data is fitted to this functional form in order to obtain estimates of the parameters of the function. Nonparametric techniques do not assume a functional form and involve estimation of the "best practices" frontier from the sample data (Lovell, 1992). While both approaches have advantages and disadvantages (see Lovell 1992, pg. 19), in this study, I use both approaches in order to triangulate the results and to gain a better understanding of the techniques. My primary research goal is to investigate the systematic contribution of IT investment to productivity (and resolve the so-called IT productivity paradox issue). I will also compare the performance of the units and find the best practices behavior using the nonparametric approach.

In the deterministic parametric approach, the production function formulation assumes that all firms convert inputs into outputs at the same level of efficiency. On the other hand, in the stochastic parametric approach, I specify an inefficiency factor for each firm so that no two firms necessarily operate at the same level of efficiency. The details of the formulations are specified in Chapter 5. With parametric techniques, we can either use the cost function approach or the production function approach. This equivalence between the cost function approach and the production function approach is due to the property of duality in the model formulations that I use in specifying the economic behavior of firms (Diewert and Wales, 1982). The cost function approach is particularly useful for testing hypotheses other than productivity such as technical progress or regress and its relation to input costs. This approach is also suitable for testing for the effects of regulation as is done in Chapter 6. The parametric production function approach provides measures such as technical efficiency and input-specific allocative inefficiency.

Nonparametric techniques are useful for determining relative efficiency of firms such as cost efficiency, technical efficiency and firm-specific allocative efficiency. By enveloping the input set from below and the output set from above, the data is enveloped by the tightest production frontier. The complete formulations and the efficiency terms are explained in greater detail in Chapter 7.

# CHAPTER 3

# The Healthcare Industry

## 3.1 INTRODUCTION

The first hospitals established in the United States were charitable institutions that cared for poverty-stricken, acutely ill patients (Rosenberg, 1987). These organizations were nonprofit and relied on donations from the wealthy for operating funds. A theme of charitable services dominated the development of these nonprofit institutions until 1950 (Johnson, 1994). After World War II, however, advances in medical technology began to have an effect on hospital operations. Then in 1965 Medicare and Medicaid began paying for much of the care that had previously been charity care, and thus provided fuel for the technology engine (Johnson, 1994). Since hospital reimbursement was on a "cost-plus" basis, financial risk rested primarily with the insurers. These factors motivated hospitals to increase costs in order to maximize revenues. After 1965, the number of hospitals and hospital beds increased and for-profit institutions began appearing (Feldstein, 1983). For the next several decades, technological developments and specialization in clinical fields helped to transform these organizations from charitable institutions into technological enterprises (Johnson, 1995). However, national health expenditures, which were 4.4 percent of GNP in 1950 and 5.9 percent in 1965, jumped to 7.4 percent by 1970 and 9.4 percent by 1980 (Fuchs, 1986). In response to this rapid increase in health care costs, Congress established a flat-fee payment system for inpatient services based on the patient diagnosis in 1983. Since some services continued to be paid on a cost-plus basis, hospitals continued to focus on revenues and developed sophisticated schemes to allocate costs so that reimbursements were maximized (Zimmerman, 1995).

In the early 1990s, hospitals began undergoing another series of changes. This era, in its early stages, appears to be a time of consolidation and competition. Within the next 15 to 20 years, a for-profit system composed of hospitals, primary care physicians, specialists, and prepayment plans has been anticipated (Johnson, 1994, p. 65). Health insurance is shifting from a cost-plus reimbursement system for any and all services used, to one where medical care is aggressively managed and controlled as well as competitively priced in a manner that determines which providers will get to serve patients. With large groups of patients up for grabs, for-profit organizations have been successful in attracting investors and expanding operations. For-profit hospitals have been buying non-profit hospitals, squeezing out excess capacities, and capitalizing on economies of scale, particularly in information systems and purchasing supplies and equipment (Flower, 1996). Cost containment has now become an important strategy in the industry (Sloan et al., 1988). With these changes, hospitals have been investing in software and hardware and overhauling their IT systems (Palley and Conger, 1995).

The healthcare industry was relatively slow in adopting information technology. Because of the emphasis on revenue maximization prior to 1983, patient billing systems were among the early uses of IT. Patient charges were delivered daily to data processing so that patient bills could be kept current and then issued shortly after discharge. Mainframe systems were used to keep patient billing and general ledger information. Smaller hospitals continued to perform these activities by hand. Because of the regulatory environment, information technology was also used intensively for regulatory reporting purposes, including budgeting. After the change in Medicare reimbursement in 1983, IT continued to be adopted for revenue enhancement, for example, sophisticated software was used to allocate costs in a manner that increased revenues from cost-plus payers (Zimmerman, 199S). Personal computers were increasingly used by individual departments for specific purposes such as inventory control in pharmacy. Automating clinical records is a relatively new objective for hospitals (Hern, 1996). Only in recent years have hospitals attempted to develop integrated cost accounting systems (Andrianos and Dykan, 1996). This dynamic operating environment offers a unique setting in which to study IT productivity.

## 3.2 REGULATION, CAPITAL INVESTMENTS, AND PERFORMANCE

The healthcare industry is a regulated industry and regulation plays an important role in determining both the capital investments undertaken and the efficiency of hospitals. Complete regulation of the health care industry and perfect market competition are polar extremes among a spectrum of solutions that have been proposed to abate the rising tide of health care costs in the US. The cost-based method of payment and administrators' desires for prestige and income maximization have resulted in inefficiencies in the demand and supply side such as duplication of expensive, prestigious services and overinvestment in capital and beds (Feldstein, 1983, p. 249). Regulation such as licensure aim at curbing or eliminating demand-side inefficiencies whereas regulation such as Certificate of Need (CON) and rate regulation are aimed at supply-side inefficiencies.

According to the economic theory of regulation (Stigler, 1971; Posner, 1974), regulatory agencies and their policies are developed by legislators to monopolize competitive markets which helps them gain more political power. Regulatory agencies wish to increase their size and authority which they accomplish by minimizing opposition. Due to high information and transaction costs, consumers rarely organize against particular legislation (see Feldstein, 1983, pp. 248–321, for a more extensive discussion of the role of regulation in the healthcare industry). It is further hypothesized that most regulation will in fact inhibit technology advances that may decrease hospital utilization and create an environment fostering monopoly pricing of hospital services. For example, CON legislation, ostensibly passed as a means of cutting hospital expenditures, was in fact a mechanism by which existing hospitals formed local cartels and erected barriers to entry so that they did not have to lower prices and forfeit revenue (Feldstein, 1983, p. 274). After the failure of CON, one of the most important legislation in this industry has been a change in reimbursement of hospital costs by the Medicare program. Reimbursement is now based on Diagnosis-Related Groupings or DRGs (Health Care Financing Administration, 1983). This system is called the Prospective Payment System, abbreviated as PPS.

The main reason for legislating PPS for Medicare patients is cost containment. While it has not yet been empirically shown that the legislation has achieved that objective, analysts have uncovered other consequences of the legislation. For example, Eldenburg and Kallapur (1997) have found that hospitals have been shifting their services to out-patient care since the implementation of PPS.

## 3.3 THE HOSPITAL AS AN ORGANIZATION

Hospitals are a major production unit of services in the healthcare indus-, try. A hospital differs from organizations in other industries in several ways.

1. Hospital organizational structure consists of two separate enti-ties: the medical staff who govern medical decision making and hospital administration who provide the services that physicians require to treat patients (Harris, 1977; Pauly and Redisch, 1973). Physicians authorize acquisition of about 80% of the capital in a hospital (Chilingerean, 1995). While they prefer to acquire the latest medical technology for high-quality patient care, adminis-trators prefer to acquire capital such as IT for administrative pur-poses.

2. The environment is highly regulated. Government legislation determines the amount and the method of reimbursement for hospitals for a large portion of patient care and thus affects the economic behavior (cost minimization, revenue maximization, etc.) of hospitals (Broom, 1988). Legislation also affects finan-cial budgeting and accounting decisions such as allocation of costs to the departments within the hospital (Zimmerman, 1995, p. 286). Furthermore, changes in accounting practices affect the design and implementation of IS software used in hospitals (Pal-ley, 1990).

3. IT is used for strategic advantage. With the growth of vertically-integrated healthcare organizations (Conrad et al., 1988) and multi-hospital systems (Sloan et al., 1992), hospital administra-tors are perceiving IT as a strategic "weapon" for internal co-or-dination and competitive advantage (Kim and Mitchelman, 1990; Henderson and Thomas, 1992).

In order to judge the effect that IT has had on hospital performance, we have to analyze the production efficiency of hospitals taking into ac-count the organization and regulation of firms in the industry (Pauly and Redisch, 1973), principal-agent problems (Newhouse, 1996) and the dominance of third-party reimbursement (Feldstein, 1983).

## 3.4 HEALTHCARE PRODUCTIVITY RESEARCH

Over the past 30 years, there has been a considerable amount of work on the productivity of hospitals. The majority of the work has been in the exploration of hospital cost functions. Breyer (1987) classified econometric studies of hospital costs as "ad hoc" and "production theoretic" studies. Studies classified as "ad hoc" simply correlate costs with possible determinants (Friedman and Pauly, 1983; Jenkins, 1980) whereas "production theoretic" studies are based on neoclassical theory of the firm (Banker et al., 1986; Vitaliano, 1987; Vita, 1990; Vitaliano and Toren, 1994). The latter approach is much preferred (Cowing et al., 1983; Vita, 1990).

Following production theory, ideally it should be possible to specify either the production function or the cost function. The production function consists of output on the left-hand side and the quantities of input on the right-hand side. Estimation of a single-equation then implies that input quantities are exogenous which is not the case. So researchers have resorted to the cost function specification in which the costs are written as a function of output quantities and input prices, both of which are exogenous. Specifying and estimating the functional form for the production or cost functions is called the parametric approach. All the studies mentioned above use the single-equation parametric approach. The estimation of production and cost functions can be made more robust by using multiequation models (see Chapter 5) and panel data techniques (see Chapter 6) as proposed by Skinner (1994).

As opposed to the parametric approach, the nonparametric approach does not require a functional specification for production function. Instead it relies on linear programming models to determine efficient firms in the sample. In the healthcare area, some of the empirical work using the nonparametric approach are Eakin (1992), Chilingerean (1995), Grosskopf et al (1995), Burgess and Wilson (1996), etc. See Lovell (1992) for a comparison between the two techniques. In this work, I provide a basis for comparison based on allocative efficiency (see Chapter 7).

Among the several contributions of this research, I attempt to (1) provide new evidence on IT productivity, (2) extend the prevailing healthcare empirical work using state-of-the-art econometric techniques including panel data, (3) test the relation between regulation and hospital costs, (4) provide triangulation between parametric and nonparametric results in productivity literature, and (5) extend the nonparametric literature by determining allocative inefficiency of firms.

CHAPTER 4
# Empirical Data

## 4.1 DATA SOURCE AND DESCRIPTION

In this chapter, we first describe the data set and then explain how variables are derived. We obtained the data (from 1976 to 1994) for this study from the Washington State Department of Health (WADOH) hospital database. We use a dataset from only one state in order to eliminate systematic state-specific biases resulting from accounting practices and healthcare policies peculiar to a state. The financial database collected by WADOH is comprised of 83 accounts divided into three different categories. Two reflect revenue generating departments: (1) those for in-patient care, primarily the board and room functions, e.g., acute care and intensive care, and (2) ancillary departments in which services are provided for both in-patients and outpatients. Examples of ancillary departments include the emergency room, pharmacy, and X-ray lab. The third

**Figure 4.1. The hospital as a production technology.**

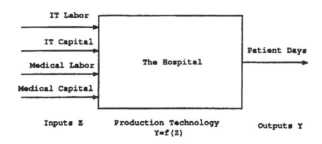

*19*

type of account reflects non–revenue generating departments (e.g., cost centers). Services such as admitting and data processing are provided by these departments. See the appendix for a list of accounts by category.

These data include charges and costs. Charges are the total dollars billed for patient services during the period and do not reflect reimbursement. Costs are the accumulated operational expenses for the period. The cost information is broken down into components such as salaries and wages, supplies, and rental expenses. In addition, charges in each revenue-generating department had to be within 105 percent of costs to be in conformance with revenue rate-setting regulation for hospitals in Washington State from 1975 to 1989. A statistical description of the sample is presented in Table 4.1. The means are larger than the medians indicating fewer large hospitals and more small, rural hospitals which is a typical pattern in Western states.

**Table 4.1. Descriptive statistics for the sample in the year 1992**

| Variable | Obs. | Mean | Median | Standard Deviation |
|---|---|---|---|---|
| Operating Revenues ($ in thousands) | 54 | 67,751 | 53,856 | 58,821 |
| Available Beds | 54 | 192 | 173 | 138 |
| Adjusted Patient-Days | 54 | 57,742 | 50,852 | 46,072 |
| Operating Cost ($ in thousands) | 54 | 58,838 | 43,725 | 55,460 |
| Operating Income ($ in thousands) | 54 | 8,912 | 7,419 | 12,243 |
| IT Capital Expense ($ in thousands) | 54 | 701 | 329 | 1,177 |
| IT Labor ($ in thousands) | 54 | 1,173 | 683 | 1,522 |
| Non-IT Capital Expense ($ in thousands) | 54 | 4,426 | 3,194 | 3,805 |
| Non-IT Labor ($ in thousands) | 54 | 31,257 | 24,213 | 27,929 |

The hospital is modeled as a production technology which uses four input factors—non-IT (or medical) labor, non-IT (or medical) capital, IT labor and IT capital—in order to produce one output, adjusted patient-days (Zweifel and Breyer, 1997, p. 271). Figure 4.1 illustrates the overview of the production process.

I classify capital expense allocated to data processing, data communication, medical records and admitting as IT capital. Capital expense in the remaining accounts is classified as non-IT capital. Total salaries from data processing and data communication are classified as IT labor. Salaries from the remaining accounts are classified as non-IT labor. In order to justify the comparison across hospitals, we retained observations of hospitals that were classified by the American Hospital Association as general medical and surgical hospitals and eliminated specialized hospitals such as psychiatric and substance abuse treatment centers from the sample. The data was checked for coding errors and inconsistencies by comparing averages over hospitals for each account for each type of expense and revenue. In some cases, missing values for the capital depreciation amount were interpolated because the capital stock calculations for each year depended on the capital depreciation amount for the previous years and missing values in the series could seriously underestimate the derived capital stock. Approximately 30 data points were generated by interpolation. Observations with coding errors and missing values were eliminated which left approximately 50+ hospital observations per year for the years 1976 to 1994, giving a total of 1064 observations.

## 4.2 MEASUREMENT ISSUES

Regardless of the level at which the productivity analysis is performed, there are difficulties and limitations in evaluating the input and output variables of the production function (Bodea, 1994). One of the most cited problems in evaluating input and output variables results from failure in capturing quality differences across the observations (year-to-year or across firms). For example, the quality of man-hour measure is not easy to take into account.

Measurements become even more difficult because the models in the previous section require *quantities* and *prices* rather than the dollar amounts of input factors since heterogeneity of input mixes across observations makes it difficult to establish *physical* units of capital inputs. Kelley (1994) suggests "previous econometric analyses assessing the impact of IT on productivity have suffered from a lack of specificity in conceptualizing the link between technology and the affected process or processes, not surprisingly, such studies find little evidence that investment in IT has had much of a payoff." This view prescribes that the unit of analysis should be the specific processes into which IT is invested to improve rather than the entire business unit. The "process-oriented" approaches echo this view (Markus and Robey, 1988, Soh and Markus, 1995). The methodological interpretation of these claims may call for analysis among more homogeneous inputs with specifically defined output (goals). Alternatively, Morrison and Berndt (1990) argue that the problem of measurement errors may be mitigated by moving toward an economy or industry level rather than a specific process or firm level because improving a process may cause inefficiency in other processes. That is, there may be some conflicts among multiple goals so that measuring gain by specific processes may ignore losses by other conflicting processes. Regardless of the level at which the analysis is performed, a shortcoming seems to be the lack (or inappropriateness) of *physical* data. To ensure comparability in production functions, commonly accepted units other than physical units such as dollar amount are often used (Mark, 1983). The next section describes how to construct "real" input and output quantities after the dollar amounts have been adjusted for inflation for the temporal comparison. In the case of IT investments, not only does inflation have to be accounted for, but also the change quality of IT capital has to be factored into its capital stock calculation. Information Technology has rapidly evolved since its inception. Especially with the introduction of powerful personal computers in early 1980s, the Bureau of Labor Statistics (BLS, 1983) has "applied" a "quality" adjustment in 1983 to IT depreciation rate. The impact of such a quality adjustment in view of a productivity analysis is to be investigated in this study.

The values for input variables in the models in the previous section are quantities (and not dollar amounts). Labor input quantities are available from the full time equivalent measure in the dataset. Since labor data is also available in dollar amounts, the price of labor can be derived for individual hospitals for each year. The salaries were deflated by the employment price index for health care services (Bureau of Statistics, 1995) to maintain compatibility over the years.

Similarly, dollar amount and quantity data for the output measure are available in the dataset. The annual charges (in dollars) by a hospital for its services reflects the output dollar measure. To calculate the output as a quantity measure, we use a derived value called adjusted patient days. Adjusted patient days is the sum of the in-patient days and the "out-patient days" derived from the inpatient days times the ratio of outpatient charges to the in-patient charges. The unit price of output is then derived as total charges divided by adjusted patient days. To adjust for the macroeconomic effects over the years, the charges were deflated by the consumer price index for health care services (WEFA, 1994).

Prior healthcare productivity studies have used proxies for input prices. For example, Zucherman et al. (1994) use the total capital expense divided by number of beds as a proxy for the price of capital faced by the individual hospital. If input prices based on sound theory are not obtained, productivity results will be unreliable. Here, the Christensen and Jorgenson (1969) formulation for asset pricing which has been used by the BLS (1983) with little revision, provides us with a means of finding good proxies for input factor prices based on microeconomic rigor. This is explained in more detail in sections 4.3 and 4.4.

## 4.3 CALCULATION OF CAPITAL STOCK

One of the aspects of the quality of data is the calculation of capital stock in IT. Capital stock is defined as the *useful* capital accumulated by the firm from past and current investments. Capital stock operationalizes the true capability of the firm in terms of productive assets, unlike annual investments which only reflect the assets acquired during a particular year (Christensen and Jorgenson, 1969).

A measure of the productive capital stock in a firm is given by

$$C_t = C_{t-1} + NI_t - D_t \tag{4.1}$$

where $C_t$, the capital stock in the current year $t$, is equal to the capital stock of the previous year $C_{t-1}$ augmented by new capital purchased in the current year $NI_t$, but decremented by some portion $D_t$ of capital that has been "retired" or depreciated.

As with most accounting data, the capital for each account in our dataset was provided in terms of their depreciated dollar amount. That is, if $100 was invested in capital in 1981, then, for a depreciation rate of 20%, the dataset would contain $20 for each year from 1981 to 1985. Each hospital may have used their own depreciation rates in preparing the financial statements. However, in order to convert the depreciated capital data back into capital stock, I assumed an appropriate common depreciation rate for all hospitals. This can be justified on the basis that financial depreciation used by individual hospitals does not reflect the actual economic depreciation. That is, continuing with the above example, in financial terms the capital purchased in 1981 is worth $0 in 1986 but in reality, the capital (plant or equipment) may well be used in the production process after 1985. In selecting the common depreciation rates, we computed depreciation rates based on the life expectancy for the capital assets (IT equipment and non-IT (medical) equipment), because the life expectancy captures the rate of retiring and obsolescence of capital. It may be argued that in a high technology area such as IT and medical technology, prices of capital calculated using a depreciation rate based on life expectancy may not reflect the decline in prices and the improvement in the quality of the equipment (in terms of speed, features, etc.) that are a consequence of a rapid growth in technology. Therefore, we could also use the quality-adjusted depreciation rate derived by WEFA (1994). By using different depreciation rates, we can determine the effects of the quality of the data, an issue emphasized in IT productivity studies (Brynjolofsson, 1993).

I used three different measures for the depreciation rates:

**Rate 1**, which equals $2/n$, where $n$ is the life expectancy (WEFA, 1994) for the asset for that year

**Rate 2**, which equals $2/n$ where $n$ is the life expectancy of the asset for 1976

**Rate 3**, which is the quality adjusted depreciation rate (WEFA, 1994) for the asset

Table 4.2 summarizes the values of the depreciation rates. Following Christensen and Jorgenson (1969) and the BLS (1983), we apply the following procedure for calculating the productive capital stock using the depreciation rate. Let $K_{t-1976}$ be the capital stock for the asset in year $t$, $d_{t-1976}$ be the depreciation rate of capital stock, and $D_{t-1976}$ be the depreciated capital stock. Then $t = -1$ represents the year 1975, and $t = 0$ represents 1976. $\tilde{D}$ represents the calculated depreciation. Assume that

$$K_{-1} = K_0/d_{-1} \tag{4.2}$$

so that

$$\tilde{D}_0 = (K_{-1} - K_{-1} \cdot d_{-1}) \cdot d_0 \tag{4.3}$$

**Table 4.2. Depreciation rates for capital stock calculation from 1977 to 1990**

| Year | IT Capital Rate 1 | IT Capital Rate 2 | IT Capital Rate 3 | Non-IT Rate 1 | Non-IT Rate 2 | Non-IT Rate 3 |
|------|------|------|------|------|------|------|
| 1976 | 0.2857 | 0.2857 | 0.0248 | 0.2004 | 0.2004 | 0.1448 |
| 1977 | 0.2857 | 0.2857 | 0.0235 | 0.2004 | 0.2004 | 0.1397 |
| 1978 | 0.2857 | 0.2857 | 0.0156 | 0.2004 | 0.2004 | 0.1349 |
| 1979 | 0.2857 | 0.2857 | 0.0403 | 0.2004 | 0.2004 | 0.1553 |
| 1980 | 0.2857 | 0.2857 | 0.0781 | 0.2004 | 0.2004 | 0.1356 |
| 1981 | 0.2857 | 0.2857 | 0.1464 | 0.2004 | 0.2004 | 0.1279 |
| 1982 | 0.4444 | 0.2857 | 0.1660 | 0.3953 | 0.2004 | 0.1072 |
| 1983 | 0.4444 | 0.2857 | 0.1701 | 0.3953 | 0.2004 | 0.1180 |
| 1984 | 0.4444 | 0.2857 | 0.2000 | 0.3953 | 0.2004 | 0.0981 |
| 1985 | 0.4444 | 0.2857 | 0.1506 | 0.3953 | 0.2004 | 0.1189 |
| 1986 | 0.4444 | 0.2857 | 0.1632 | 0.3953 | 0.2004 | 0.1289 |
| 1987 | 0.4444 | 0.2857 | 0.2119 | 0.3953 | 0.2004 | 0.1036 |
| 1988 | 0.4000 | 0.2857 | 0.1827 | 0.2635 | 0.2004 | 0.1185 |
| 1989 | 0.4000 | 0.2857 | 0.1939 | 0.2635 | 0.2004 | 0.1168 |
| 1990 | 0.4000 | 0.2857 | 0.2011 | 0.2635 | 0.2004 | 0.1180 |
| 1991 | 0.4000 | 0.2857 | 0.1916 | 0.2635 | 0.2004 | 0.1081 |
| 1992 | 0.4000 | 0.2857 | 0.2115 | 0.2635 | 0.2004 | 0.1282 |
| 1993 | 0.4000 | 0.2857 | 0.2071 | 0.2635 | 0.2004 | 0.1251 |
| 1994 | 0.4000 | 0.2857 | 0.1882 | 0.2635 | 0.2004 | 0.1069 |

Then we can write

$$I_0 = \begin{cases} D_0 - \tilde{D}_0/d_0, & \text{if } D_0 >= \tilde{D}_0; \\ 0, & \text{otherwise.} \end{cases} \qquad (4.4)$$

So that

$$K_0 = (K_{-1} - K_{-1} \cdot d_{-1}) + I_0 \qquad (4.5)$$

Now, the algorithm can be applied recursively to all future years to establish the capital stock in each year. Thus, for any year $t$ in the future,

$$\tilde{D}_{t-1976} = (K_{t-1977} - K_{t-1977}d_{t-1977}) \cdot d_{t-1976} \cdot \tag{4.6}$$

Then

$$I_{t-1976} = \begin{cases} D_{t-1976} - \tilde{D}_{t-1976}/d_{t-1976}, & \text{if } D_{t-1976} >= \tilde{D}_{t-1976}; \\ 0, & \text{otherwise.} \end{cases} \tag{4.7}$$

Finally,

$$K_{t-1976} = (K_{t-1977} - K_{t-1977} \cdot d_{t-1977}) + K_{t-1976} \cdot \tag{4.8}$$

Hereafter, the data containing the capital stock calculated using the depreciation rate based on the variable life expectancy rate (Rate 1) is called Data 1, the data containing the capital stock calculated using the rate from based on the constant life expectancy (Rate 2) is called Data 2, and that calculated from the quality-adjusted rate (Rate 3) is called Data 3. To measure the first year's stocks correctly, it is necessary to collect historical investment data extending back as long as the life of the asset. Since the data for the productive capital stock prior to 1975 was not available, the capital stock for the beginning few years may be "noisy." However, the span of 18 years of data covers the life expectancy of both IT and medical equipment. Therefore, it is reasonable to conclude that the capital stock thus derived would eventually have stabilized and converged to less noisy capital stock values in successive years.

## 4.4 PRICES AND QUANTITIES OF INPUT FACTORS

As stated, theoretical models in section 3 require *quantities* and *prices* of input variables. For analysis at the firm level and beyond, it is extremely difficult to construct "physical" units of capital investment. Therefore, instead of using the "physical" units price of capital inputs, the "implicit rental price" or "user cost" of capital are formulated, based on "the neoclassical principle that inputs should be aggregated using weights that reflect their marginal products" (Bureau of Labor Statistics, 1983). BLS states:

The assumption used to formulate the rental price expression is that the purchase price of a capital asset equals the discounted value of the stream of services (and, hence, implicitly the rents) that the asset will provide.

Disregarding inflation and taxes, the rental price, $p_{it}$, would be

$$p_{it} = q_t(r_{it} + d_t) \tag{4.9}$$

where $q_t$ is the price index of the asset for the year $t$, $r_{it}$ is an annual rate of return for unit $i$ which depends on the income and expenses for the unit, and $d_t$ is the annual depreciation rate. The economic implication in equation 4.9 is that "user cost" $p_{it}$ represents "the amount of rent that would have to be charged in order to cover costs of $q_t$ dollars' worth of an asset" (BLS, 1983) based on the firm's rational decision to "buy or rent." Since the rate of return depends on the income and capital stock available, the derived proxies for prices will vary from hospital to hospital over the years and hence, satisfy the condition that the prices be independent variables that are exogenously determined. Inflation in the prices of new assets and tax laws complicate the derivation of the rental price and "implicit" rate of return. The following set of equations describe how the rate of return and prices are calculated from the aforementioned general formulation. The method used to obtain the "user costs" of assets is based on Christensen and Jorgenson (1969).

To determine the capital prices, we use the Christensen and Joorgenson (1969) formulation to derive the price $p_i$ of the $i$th input factor (IT capital or non-IT capital) given by

$$p_{iA}{}^t = q_A{}^{t-1} r_i{}^t + q_A{}^t d_A{}^t - (q_A{}^t - q_A{}^{t-1}) \tag{4.10}$$

where $q_A{}^t$ is the price index of asset $A$ for the year $t$, $r_i{}^t$ is the rate of return for the hospital $i$ for the year $t$, and $d_A{}^t$ is the depreciation rate of the asset $A$ for the year $t$. The rate of return for the hospital is calculated by

$$r_i{}^t = \frac{(I_i{}^t - \sum^2_{A=1}[p_{iA}{}^t * d_A{}^t * C_{iA}{}^t - (p_{iA}{}^t - p_{iA}{}^{t-1}) * C_{iA}{}^t])}{\sum^2_{A=1}[p_{iA}{}^{t-1} * C_{iA}{}^t]} \tag{4.11}$$

where $I_i{}^t$ is the capital income defined by revenues minus operating expenses and $C_{iA}{}^t$ is the capital stock in asset $A$ for the unit $i$ for the year $t$. $A = 1$ stands for IT capital, and $A = 2$ stands for non-IT capital. The price indices $q_A^t$ and the rates of depreciation $d_A^t$ were obtained from WEFA 1994.

The IT and non-IT prices thus derived are plotted as graphs in Figures 4.2 and 4.3, respectively. The values are presented in Table 4.3. It is noteworthy that different depreciation rates result in significant differences in the input prices. Therefore, an opportunity arises to present a sensitivity analysis of the "quality" issues mentioned before. Finally, having determined the input factor prices, the annual input quantities for

**Figure 4.2. Average IT capital prices over time**

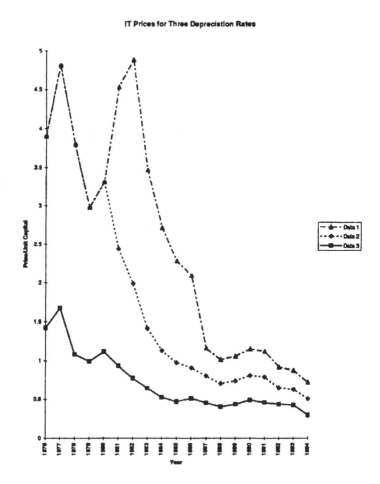

IT Prices for Three Depreciation Rates

capital for each hospital are determined by dividing the capital in dollar amounts by the derived prices.

## 4.5 ADVANTAGES OF THE DATASET

This data set has several advantages over data sets employed in previous IT productivity studies. First, due to the regulatory nature of data collec-

**Figure 4.3. Average non-IT (medical) capital over time.**

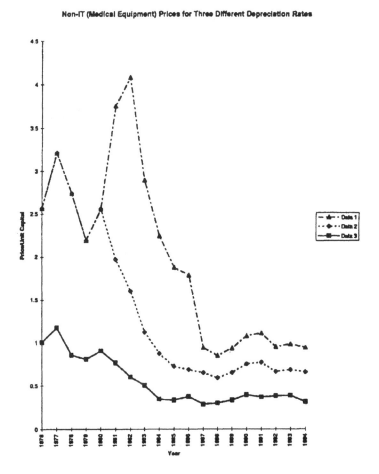

Non-IT (Medical Equipment) Prices for Three Different Depreciation Rates

**Table 4.3. Prices of IT and non-IT capital from 1976 to 1994**

| Year | Sample Size | Medical Capital Price | IT Capital Price |
|------|------------|----------------------|------------------|
| 1976 | 49 | 1.0070 (0.5856) | 1.4217 (0.8738) |
| 1977 | 56 | 1.1736 (0.7485) | 1.6776 (1.0940) |
| 1978 | 57 | 0.8559 (0.5628) | 1.0836 (0.7617) |
| 1979 | 56 | 0.8974 (0.4702) | 0.9911 (0.6156) |
| 1980 | 56 | 0.9053 (0.4414) | 1.1182 (0.5522) |
| 1981 | 55 | 0.7643 (0.3619) | 0.9364 (0.4319) |
| 1982 | 57 | 0.6015 (0.2543) | 0.7747 (0.3009) |
| 1983 | 59 | 0.5052 (0.3096) | 0.6499 (0.3657) |
| 1984 | 57 | 0.3477 (0.2293) | 0.5282 (0.2716) |
| 1985 | 63 | 0.3356 (0.2088) | 0.4695 (0.2453) |
| 1986 | 63 | 0.3754 (0.2517) | 0.5164 (0.2825) |
| 1987 | 60 | 0.2877 (0.1769) | 0.4567 (0.1859) |
| 1988 | 59 | 0.3024 (0.1945) | 0.4070 (0.1945) |
| 1989 | 55 | 0.3348 (0.2213) | 0.4379 (0.2113) |
| 1990 | 53 | 0.3950 (0.2430) | 0.4939 (0.2208) |
| 1991 | 54 | 0.3687 (0.2267) | 0.4590 (0.1929) |
| 1992 | 54 | 0.3814 (0.2593) | 0.4393 (0.2031) |
| 1993 | 51 | 0.3872 (0.2685) | 0.4279 (0.1918) |
| 1994 | 50 | 0.3130 (0.2174) | 0.2983 (0.1367) |

tion, hospitals are required to report accounts for IT expenses separately from other capital which is, in general, not found in financial statement information. Prior studies have resorted to ex-ante surveying in order to obtain data for IT expense items and it is not clear how reliably those numbers have been reported by the respondents. Secondly, it is still controversial whether meaningful inferences can be drawn from empirical studies using data sets containing observations from heterogeneous firms. For example, the MPIT data set studied by Loveman (1994), and Lee and Barua (1996) covers six different subsectors in manufacturing and Brynjolofsson and Hitt (1996) use a dataset from many different sectors. The data set used in this study, however, contains a highly homogeneous set of observations. Furthermore, the units of analysis in several other studies were subunits of firms which included allocation of expenses by the headquarters. Cost allocations do not necessarily reflect the use of resources and thus are prone to poor quality of data problems. This data set does not suffer from these shortcomings. Finally, productivity analysis requires precise measures of the capital stock inputs which are not easily captured through "snapshot" financial statements. For this, we need a time window that at a minimum covers the life expectancy of capital input. Most data that were used in previous research did not have such a wide time window, whereas this dataset covers 18 years.

## 4.6 CONTROL VARIABLES

Even within a data set with seemingly homogeneous units, there are confounds due to the effect of other organizational factors (Kimberly and Evanisko, 1981). Some of the major confounding effects in a hospital productivity study are ownership structure (Burgess and Wilson, 1996), case mix (which reflects patient severity), teaching status, and time effect. Ownership was not a major confound in the dataset because the majority of hospitals in Washington are nonprofit (about 92 percent), which have uniformly enjoyed tax benefits and similar costs of capital. It is also possible that among the nonprofit hospitals there could be organizational differences between state-owned, county-owned, and church-owned hospitals, but I ignore these confounds for this research. Since the data represent an eighteen-year period during which several technology advances and policy changes occurred in the healthcare industry, a control variable for the time effect was added. Since there were an average of 10 teaching hospitals in the sample each year, I tested the sensitivity of the results to the addition of a dummy variable in the production function controlling for the teaching status of hospitals. The time effect and teaching status control variables were applied to the production function approach given in the next chapter because the data were pooled over the years. In Chapter 6, since I use panel data techniques to isolate firmwise and yearwise effects, I do not use any control variables for time or teaching status. The data analysis in Chapter 7 was conducted for each year separately and only nonteaching hospitals were included in the analysis. While this might create difficulties in direct comparison of some of the results using the different techniques, the results can be better interpreted without the presence of confounding effects.

# CHAPTER 5

# Production Theory and Productivity Analysis

## 5.1 BACKGROUND AND BEHAVIORAL ASSUMPTIONS

In a productivity study, a behavioral model is ascribed to all firms in the sample and estimates of parameters are determined which best fit the model. For example, in current healthcare research, there is evidence of cost minimization behavior by hospitals (Sloan et al., 1988). Indeed, cost minimization will necessarily hold true (though it is not sufficient) for many alternative behavioral models such as growth maximization, budget maximization or profit maximization (Cowing et al., 1983).

We are concerned with behavioral assumptions because these behavioral assumptions dictate how realistic the estimation models are. Firms maximize profits or minimize costs subject to their production technology constraints. So if the model we estimate does not reflect this managerial behavior and does not utilize the full information provided by the system of equations thus derived, the estimates of the parameters of the production function will not be consistent and cannot be usefully interpreted (Greene, 1993, p. 578).[1] Consider a cost minimization behavioral model given by

$$\min_{\bar{z}} \bar{w} \cdot \bar{z}$$
$$\text{s.t. } \bar{y} = f(\bar{z}), \tag{5.1}$$

---

[1] See Greene 1993, pg. 616, where it is shown that a system of equations methods dominate least-squares methods.

where $\bar{w} = (w_1, ..., w_n)$ is the vector of $n$ input prices, $\bar{z} = (z_1, ..., z_n)$ is the vector of inputs, $\bar{y} = (y_1, ..., y_m)$ is the vector of outputs and $f(\bar{z})$ is the correspondence[2] that defines the production technology. $f(\bar{z})$ quantifies the feasible quantities of outputs that can be produced from given quantities of inputs $\bar{z}$.

As we can see, the cost minimization problem is formulated such that input quantities are endogenous (decision) variables whereas the corresponding prices are exogenous. That is, firms do not decide on the prices of the inputs; the input markets do that. Firms do, however, decide on how much of each input quantity should be bought or acquired. Pitfalls that we encounter when we try to estimate a production function by regressing output quantity over input dollar amounts (expenditure) are well documented (Varian, 1984, pp. 171–176). Lee and Barua (1995) maintain that some previous IS productivity studies have ignored this fundamental methodological issue resulting in a failure to ascertain a productivity gain by IT investment. In order to estimate the model based on this optimization assumption, we need **quantities** and **prices** of inputs. It is important that the prices of inputs should vary across firms in order to be considered independent variables in regression models.

## 5.2 EMPIRICAL MODEL AND ESTIMATION

To solve equation 5.1, we rewrite it using the Lagrange multiplier ($\lambda$) technique, as

$$\min_{\bar{z},\lambda}[\bar{w}\cdot\bar{z} - \lambda(\bar{y} - f(\bar{z}))]. \tag{5.2}$$

Differentiating equation (5.2) with respect to each $z_i$ and $\lambda$ gives the first-order conditions which, combined with the original production function, yields the following system of equations:

$$\bar{y} = f(\bar{z}) \tag{5.3}$$

$$\frac{f_i(\bar{z})}{f_j(\bar{z})} = \frac{w_i}{w_j} \quad \forall i = 1,...,n, \ i \neq j, \tag{5.4}$$

---

[2] $f(\bar{z})$ is called the production function when $\bar{y}$ is single-valued and not a set.

where $f_k(\overline{z})$ refers to the partial of $f(\overline{z})$ with respect to $z_k$. Equations 5.3 and 5.4 represent a set of $n$ equations—one equation for the production function and the second set containing $n-1$ equations. The $n-1$ equations embody the microeconomic intuition that in an equilibrium situation, a firm will equate the ratio of marginal product of an input and its price for all input factors to a common ratio. Using suitable functional forms for $f(\overline{z})$, the above system of equations can be written explicitly in terms of the parameters of the production correspondence. The following section outlines the forms of the production function that are commonly used and that we use in this study. The Full Information Maximum Likelihood (FIML) method can then be applied on the resulting equations to yield consistent and most efficient estimates of the parameters (Greene, 1993, p. 612). FIML is especially useful for specifying that the output is exogenous (because the amount of service provided by a hospital is subject to great uncertainty, McClellan 1995) while the inputs are endogenous to the production system; i.e., the decision regarding the quantities of input factors is made within the hospital. Once the production function is estimated, the impact $E_i$ of any input $z_i$ is determined by simply differentiating the function $f(\overline{z})$ with respect to the input factor $z_i$. That is,

$$E_i = \frac{\partial f(\overline{z})}{\partial z_i} \cdot \quad (5.5)$$

While studying IT productivity, the data is aggregated such that the input factors are $\overline{z}$ = (IT capital, non-IT capital, IT-related labor, non-IT labor) and the output quantity $\overline{y}$ is expressed in appropriate manufacturing or service output units. As mentioned earlier, capital stock is defined as the useful capital accumulated over the years which is a measure of the capital used in the current production process.

### 5.2.1 Using Deterministic Production Functions

A Cobb-Douglas function represents constant returns to scale production technology and is given by

$$\overline{y} = \left( \prod_{i=1}^{n} z_i^{a_i} \right) e^{bt} e^{cD} \quad (5.6)$$

where the $n$ inputs factors are $z_i$ and, $a_i$, $b$ and $D$ are the parameters that characterize the production function. The time effect is controlled by the variable $t$ and its nonzero coefficient $b$ (thereby capturing the dis-embedded technical change). The parameter for the dummy organizational variable $D$ is $c$. Substituting equation 5.6 into equations 5.3 and 5.4, we obtain a system of equations which, as mentioned earlier, can by estimated by FIML. The impact of the input factors can now be determined by substituting equation 5.6 after it has been estimated in equation 5.5 as

$$E_i = a_i \frac{y}{z_i} \quad \forall i = 1,\ldots,n. \quad (5.7)$$

Equation 5.7 uses the output and input quantities rather than expenditures. A measure of the impact on the revenues with respect to the expenditures can be written as

$$E_i' = a_i \frac{y \cdot p_y}{w_i \cdot z_i} \quad \forall i = 1,\ldots,n. \quad (5.8)$$

### 5.2.2 Using Stochastic Production Frontiers

The possibility of mismanagement in Information Systems has been often cited (Brynjolofsson, 1993) and the limitations of deterministic approaches in IT business value measurement are criticized by Soh and Markus (1995). Factors such as firmwise mismanagement, differences in IT expertise and maturity among firms, etc., can be modeled using stochastic production frontiers. Stochastic production frontiers use the same basic formulations as presented in the previous section. In addition, inefficiency terms are introduced into each of the equations. That is, equations 5.3 and 5.4 are now rewritten with the stochastic inefficiency terms as (Schmidt and Lovell, 1979)—

$$\bar{y} = f(\bar{z})e^{(v-u)}, \quad (5.9)$$

$$\frac{f_i(\bar{z})}{f_j(\bar{z})} = \frac{w_i}{w_j} e^{\epsilon i}, \quad \forall i = 1,\ldots,n, \text{ and } i \neq j, \quad (5.10)$$

where $u$ is the technical inefficiency of a firm, $v$ is random statistical noise and $\epsilon_i$ is the allocative inefficiency for input $i$. There are $n-1$ allocative inefficiency factors since there are $n$ input factors and $n-1$ independent allocation equations. $u$ is assumed to follow a normal distribution truncated below zero with a standard deviation of $\sigma_u$. The standard deviation of $v$ is $\sigma_v$, and $v$ also is normally distributed. $\epsilon_i$ is also normally distributed with a standard deviation of $\sigma_\epsilon$. With an additional assumption that these random variables ($u$, $v$, and $\epsilon$) are independent, Schmidt and Lovell (1979) present an estimation procedure based on "concentrating" the maximum likelihood function derived from the joint probability distribution of the sum of the error terms.

**Estimation procedure.** The error term in equation (5.9) is the sum of a truncated normal distribution and a full normal distribution. The error terms $\epsilon_i$ in equation 5.10 can be assumed to follow a normal multivariate distribution with mean vector $\mu$ and a standard deviation matrix $\Sigma$. The log likelihood function is derived as given in Schmidt and Lovell (1979). The estimation burden of estimating the parameters of the production function, $\sigma_v$, $\sigma_u$, and $\mu$, and $\Sigma$ can be eased by concentrating the log likelihood function with respect to $\mu$ and $\Sigma$. To do that we first assume the starting values of the estimates for $\mu$ and $\Sigma$ by calculating the error terms of equation 5.4 as determined by the deterministic formulation. The maximum likelihood estimates for the stochastic formulation can now be obtained for the remaining parameters by keeping $\mu$ and $\Sigma$ constant. The parameter estimates thus obtained can be inserted into equation 5.10 and new estimates for $\mu$ and $\Sigma$ can be calculated. This procedure was iterated several times until the parameter estimates, on visual inspection, converged without numerical problems and with reasonable $t$-statistic values.

Equations 5.9 and 5.10 present a very realistic picture of hospital operations by explicitly modeling two factors:

1. No two firms can produce the same level of output using identical levels of input such as IT resources (Weill, 1992). This difference between firm $k$ and the "ideal" (given by the production function) in converting inputs to outputs is called technical inefficiency $u_k$ (such that $u_k > 0$).
2. No firm will necessarily allocate resources at the optimal level given by the first order condition of cost minimization (see equation 5.4). The allocative inefficiency, $\epsilon_i$, measures the difference between the actual allocation from the optimal allocation (see equation 5.10).

## 5.3 RESULTS AND DISCUSSIONS

### 5.3.1 IT Capital Investment Contributions

Table 5.1 contains estimates and standard errors (in parenthesis) of the parameters of the deterministic model. Table 5.4 reports those for the stochastic model. Table 5.1 provides evidence of the sign or direction of the impact of the input factors. Note that the impacts of IT capital, non-IT capital, and non-IT labor are all positive, whereas the impact of IT labor is negative. The magnitudes of the means of the impacts are estimated by equation 5.7, which uses the parameter estimates given above and the ratio of output quantity to input quantity. Referring to Table 5.2, the magnitude of the mean impact of IT capital is larger than the magnitude of the mean impact of non-IT capital. While the standard deviations of the impacts of IT capital, IT labor, and non-IT capital vary greatly over the sample, the standard deviation of the impact of non-IT labor indicates a much lower dispersion.

**Table 5.1. Parameter estimates from deterministic formulation**

| Variable | *without Teach Control* | | | *with Teach Control* | | |
|---|---|---|---|---|---|---|
|  | Data 1 | Data 2 | Data 3 | Data 1 | Data 2 | Data 3 |
| Constant | 3.1919 | 2.3201 | 0.4775 | 2.7279 | 1.6869 | −0.6256 |
|  | (0.0902) | (0.1991) | (0.1813) | (0.0709) | (0.1396) | (0.3245)[1] |
| Non-IT labor | 0.8677 | 0.7940 | 0.6339 | 0.9267 | 0.8589 | 0.7064 |
|  | (0.0128) | (0.0283) | (0.0172) | (0.0088) | (0.0189) | (0.0334) |
| Non-IT Capital | 0.1750 | 0.2538 | 0.3669 | 0.1869 | 0.2741 | 0.4082 |
|  | (0.0026) | 0.0036) | (0.0059) | (0.0028) | (0.0042) | (0.0073) |
| IT labor | −0.0166 | −0.0152 | −0.0121 | −0.0177 | −0.0164 | −0.0135 |
|  | (0.0004) | (0.0009) | (0.0005) | (0.0003) | (0.005) | (0.008) |
| IT Capital | 0.0085 | 0.0121 | 0.0643 | 0.0091 | 0.0131 | 0.0707 |
|  | (0.0002) | (0.0005) | (0.0040) | (0.0003) | (0.0004) | (0.0066) |
| Time Trend | −0.0525 | −0.0611 | −0.0835 | −0.0553 | −0.0641 | −0.0893 |
|  | (0.0015) | (0.0019) | (0.0028) | (0.0015) | (0.0022) | (0.0032) |
| Teach |  |  |  | −0.2625 | −0.3167 | −0.4437 |
|  |  |  |  | (0.0278) | (0.0412) | (0.0630) |

[1] Not significant. P-value is less than 0.0005 for all other estimates.

**Table 5.2. Marginal productivity of inputs from the deterministic formulation**

| Variable | without Teach Control | | | with Teach Control | | |
|---|---|---|---|---|---|---|
| | Data 1 | Data 2 | Data 3 | Data 1 | Data 2 | Data 3 |
| IT Capital | 0.0141 | 0.0122 | 0.0024 | 0.0151 | 0.0132 | 0.0027 |
| | (0.0274) | (0.0336) | (0.0052) | (0.0293) | (0.0363) | (0.0058) |
| Non-IT Capital | 0.0089 | 0.0064 | 0.0021 | 0.0096 | 0.0069 | 0.0023 |
| | (0.0125) | (0.0112) | (0.0040) | (0.0133) | (0.0121) | (0.0044) |
| IT Labor | −76.507 | −70.049 | −55.867 | −81.715 | −75.775 | −62.256 |
| | (129.1) | (118.3) | (94.4) | (131.3) | (127.9) | (105.2) |
| Non-IT Labor | 74.310 | 67.996 | 54.288 | 79.359 | 73.556 | 60.497 |
| | (16.130) | (14.759) | (11.750) | (17.226) | (15.967) | (13.094) |

[1] For all values, p-value is less than 0.0005.

While Table 5.2 gives the relative mean marginal productivity contribution or the mean change in output quantity for a unit increase in the input quantity, equation 5.8 can be used to generate the mean marginal revenue contribution or the mean change in the revenue for a unit change in the input expenditure. Table 5.3 lists the values. Examining these values, we see that in dollar amounts both IT capital and non-IT capital have large average influences on revenue generation. At the same time, the large standard deviations for IT capital and labor lead to the observation that there is a large variation in the firmwise impact of IT capital and labor on the revenues. For example, in Data 3 with a control variable for teaching status, the minimum impact value was 0.1050 and the maximum was 47.1150. This provides evidence of the importance of IT conversion effectiveness differences between firms as postulated by Weill (1992). We do not see a large variation in the use of non-IT capital or non-IT labor such as medical equipment over the sample, perhaps because the primary business of hospitals is providing healthcare services and hospitals have achieved considerable expertise in the utilization of medical equipment and professionals over a long learning period, whereas the industry-wide variation in IT capital and labor effectiveness indicates that organizational learning in hospitals with regard to IT is still in its infancy.

As discussed earlier, the variations between firms in efficiently using the production technology and in allocating input proportionately

**Table 5.3. Marginal revenue contribution of inputs from deterministic formulation**

| Variable | without Teach Control | | | with Teach Control | | |
|---|---|---|---|---|---|---|
| | Data 1 | Data 2 | Data 3 | Data 1 | Data 2 | Data 3 |
| IT Capital | 2.7925 | 2.5605 | 2.5226 | 2.9822 | 2.7669 | 2.8140 |
| | (3.3758) | (2.9683) | (3.2789) | (3.6051) | (3.2077) | (3.6577) |
| Non-IT Capital | 2.0474 | 1.8556 | 1.5530 | 2.1865 | 2.0044 | 1.7276 |
| | (1.2091) | (1.0433) | (1.0292) | (1.2913) | (1.1270) | (1.1449) |
| IT Labor | −2.4782 | −2.2689 | −1.8104 | −2.6472 | −2.4549 | −2.0174 |
| | (4.8638) | (4.4532) | (3.5529) | (5.1955) | (4.8182) | (3.9592) |
| Non-IT Labor | 1.9950 | 1.8256 | 1.4578 | 2.1308 | 1.9751 | 1.6244 |
| | (0.3299) | (0.3019) | (0.2413) | (0.3524) | (0.3567) | (0.2688) |

[1] For all values, p-value is less than 0.0005.

to prices is not entirely random. The error terms include systematic mismanagement and under- or overutilization of inputs. The stochastic frontier captures this variation. The results of the stochastic frontier parameter estimation given by equations 5.9 and 5.10 are presented in Table 5.4. The impacts derived thereof are presented in Table 5.5.

The results in Table 5.5 are similar to those obtained from the deterministic formulation. They show a consistent direction of the impact for all of the inputs for the three data sets. IT capital exhibits a positive influence in all three data sets. IT labor, on the other hand, shows a negative impact in the data sets. I explore this issue in section 5.3. Non-IT-related labor exhibits a positive influence when there is small variation among sample units. This can be attributed to the fact that salary expenses of healthcare employees such as nurses and technicians are directly correlated to high revenues.

### 5.3.2 Quality Adjustment

In order to determine the effect of quality adjustment on capital data, we find the ratio of the parameter estimates of the input factor for Data 2 and 3 with respect to Data 1 parameter estimates. Table 5.6 gives the resulting ratios (as a percentage) from the deterministic and stochastic formulations.

**Table 5.4. Parameter estimates from stochastic production frontier**

| Parameter[1] | Data 1 | Data 2 | Data 3 |
|---|---|---|---|
| Constant | 4.5119 | 4.4809 | 4.3766 |
| | (.0379) | (.0382) | (.0399) |
| Non-IT labor $(a_1)$ | 1.0520 | 1.0506 | 1.0395 |
| | (.0069) | (.0069) | (0.0070) |
| Non-IT Capital $(a_2)$ | 0.0081 | 0.0109 | 0.0140 |
| | (.0002) | (.0002) | (.0003) |
| IT labor $(a_3)$ | –0.0132 | –0.0136 | –0.0080 |
| | (.0002) | (.0002) | (.0001) |
| IT Capital $(a_4)$ | 0.0011 | 0.0010 | 0.0077 |
| | (3e-5) | (2e-5) | (.0003) |
| Time Trend $(a_t)$ | –.0341 | –.0350 | –0.0354 |
| | (.0009) | (.0009) | (.0009) |
| Teach $(c)$ | –.1451 | –.1466 | –.1569 |
| | (.0185) | (.0188) | (.0191) |
| Technical Inefficiency $(\sigma_u)$ | –.1817 | .1822 | .1842 |
| | (.0064) | (.0066) | (.0069) |
| Allocative Inefficiencies $(\sigma_v)$ | .0096 | .1007 | .1020 |
| | (.0037) | (.0037) | (.0039) |

[1] For all values, p is less than 0.0005.

We see that quality adjustment in the depreciation rate of capital has the effect of making it more "valuable" in terms of productivity. In other words, by not applying the quality adjustment to capital data, we seriously underestimate the parameter estimates that determine the productivity contribution. For example, IT capital is underestimated by over seven times when quality-adjusted data are not used. The use of a stochastic production frontier reduces this difference by 50 percent. We also see that IT capital is more affected by quality adjustment than is non-IT capital. This may be because of the rapid development in IT technology compared to non IT technology such as medical equipment. In the IT industry, the performance of hardware has risen rapidly while hardware prices have declined. In the IT industry, quality adjustment of capital also reflects the fact that PCs and powerful desktops in a networked envi-

**Table 5.5. Marginal revenue contribution of inputs from stochastic formulation**

| Factor | Data 1 | Data 2 | Data 3 |
|---|---|---|---|
| IT Capital | 0.3458 | 0.2159 | .3070 |
|  | (.4180) | (.2504) | (.3991) |
| Non-IT Capital | .0950 | .0797 | .0594 |
|  | (.0561) | (.0448) | (.0394) |
| IT Labor | −1.9702 | −2.0252 | −1.2019 |
|  | (3.8669) | (3.9747) | (2.3588) |
| Non-IT Labor | 2.4191 | 2.4158 | 2.3904 |
|  | (.4001) | (.3998) | (.3956) |

ronment are quickly replacing mammoth mainframes. Although the performance of medical equipment has risen (such as availability of sophisticated equipment such as magnetic resonance imagers), the prices have remained relatively high.

### 5.3.3 IT Labor

The parameter estimate reflecting the impact of IT labor shows a negative contribution to the productivity of hospitals. I reason that, in the period under investigation, hospitals were investing more in IT capital and at the same time the healthcare industry was undergoing several environmental changes which required overhauling of IT too often, leading to seemingly excessive use of IT labor in any particular year. This could cause the IT labor input to drive its contribution to production in the negative direction when analyzed in an econometric model. Furthermore, not all IT labor is accounted for in the data because of missing information on the outsourcing activities of hospitals in our sample. It is possible that by factoring in the expenditure due to outsourcing, IT labor may show a positive contribution as the average behavior of the firms. In previous research, allowing that the "fruits" of IT labor are realized over the years following such investment, researchers have justified increasing the annual IT labor input by a multiplicative factor (for example, Hitt and Brynjolofsson, 1996, justify using a factor of 3). This derived IT labor value represents "labor stock" and is added to the IT capital value for an aggregate measure of IT used in the production process.

**Table 5.6. Percentage change in parameter estimates
using quality adjusted data**

| Parameter | *Normalized Parameter Estimates* | | | |
|---|---|---|---|---|
| | *Deterministic* | | *Stochastic* | |
| | Data 2 | Data 3 | Data 2 | Data 3 |
| IT Capital | 144 | 777 | 97 | 733 |
| Non IT Capital | 147 | 365 | 134 | 173 |
| IT Labor | 92 | 76 | 103 | 61 |
| Non IT Labor | 92 | 76 | 99 | 98 |

In Table 5.7, I present results of aggregating IT labor multiplied by a factor of 3 and adding it to the IT capital value to create one IT investment measure. The formulation follows the deterministic approach that was described in section 5.2.1.

Note that all parameter estimates are consistent in their signs. Focusing on the parameter estimate corresponding to IT, we note that the estimates in Table 5.7 are close in the order of magnitude to the estimates from the deterministic formulation with disaggregated IT capital and labor values given in Table 5.1. This indicates that if there were no particular interest in eliciting productivity impacts of IT capital and IT labor separately, IT labor and capital could be aggregated into one measure as has been done in previous studies, and still yield reliable results.

### 5.3.4 Teaching and Multiple Objectives

In Table 5.1, the dummy variable used for teaching status consistently reflects a negative influence on production of services regardless of the specification. I conclude that when a control for teaching status is not used, the estimates of the parameters are underestimated. The lower productivity of teaching hospitals probably indicates a tendency to overutilize labor and capital in order to train physicians and interns (such as assigning several paid interns to one patient), thereby resulting in lower productivity from resource utilization. Because my model rather myopically considers only one objective, cost minimization, and only one output, revenues, one cannot infer how productively teaching hospitals achieve a different set of goals, namely providing healthcare services and

**Table 5.7. Estimates of parameters using aggregate IT measure**

| Input Factor | Data 1 | | Data 2 | | Data 3 | |
|---|---|---|---|---|---|---|
| Constant | 2.5814 | (.0961) | 1.6055 | (.1302) | −.7600 | (.2187) |
| IT | .0600 | (.0012) | .0615 | (.0013) | .1159 | (.0036) |
| Non IT Capital | .1769 | (.0037) | .2593 | (.0053) | .3873 | (.0098) |
| Non IT Labor | .8645 | (.0097) | .8014 | (.0109) | .6614 | (.0122) |
| Time | −.0611 | (.0019) | −.0706 | (.0028) | −.0897 | (.0044) |
| Teaching Status | −.2694 | (.0325) | −.3150 | (.0394) | −.4300 | (.0534) |

producing quality healthcare professionals. This study validates extant hypotheses that organizational variables such as teaching status do affect hospitals overall (e.g., Kimberly and Evanisko, 1981). Similarly, in various industries in which IT productivity is being determined, different organizational variables will have the effect of either overestimating or underestimating productivity contribution. This means that future productivity research must carefully consider multiobjective and multioutput models in order to determine the reliable impacts of input factors.

# CHAPTER 6

# Policy Changes and IT Investments

## 6.1 REGULATIONS IN THE HEALTHCARE INDUSTRY

The Diagnosis-Related Grouping (DRG) based Prospective Payment System (PPS) for reimbursement of medical costs of Medicare patients was enacted in 1983 by the federal government as a means of cost containment. National health expenditures had risen from 4.4 percent of GNP in 1950 to 9.4 percent of the GNP in 1980 (Fuchs, 1986). This reimbursement system provided incentives for major changes in hospital management. The most important change was that hospitals moved from revenue maximization to a cost minimization strategy (Sloan, Morrisey, and Valvona, 1988). By paying a fixed fee for a diagnosis irrespective of the actual charges incurred, the government forced hospitals to find cheaper ways to provide for patient care. Organizational changes such as vertical integration and the formation of HMOs are also altering the cost structure of patient care (Newhouse, 1996). Newhouse (1996, p. 1238) claims that managed care has led to the reduction of moral hazard in healthcare services. In the traditional healthcare environment, consumers selected inefficient health providers because they did not have an incentive to search for a better provider. This led to a patient care cost structure that enabled providers to maximize reimbursements which did not reduce costs. That was prior to legislation such as PPS. The situation now may be different. The goal of this chapter is to empirically analyze the behavior of hospital costs in an attempt to shed light on changes caused by regulation. The analysis is based on the estimation of a cost function for a group of hospitals from a single state (a highly homogeneous sample). Based on the cost function obtained, I determine: (1) the responsiveness of total hospital cost to the prices of IT, medical capital, and labor; (2) the rate of technical change in the industry and whether the change was IT-, medical capital-, or labor-using; (3) substitution and complementarity effects between the input factors; and, finally, (4) the effect of regulation on hospital costs, on substitution effects between inputs and on the rate of technical change. This approach is complementary to the production function approach used to assess the contribution of IT to productivity in the previous chapter, but is more versatile in analysis relating to regulation and capital/labor costs.

The estimation technique in this chapter differs from the previous chapter in its use of the panel data technique. The data set is the same that was constructed in Chapter 4. Note that the data set forms an unbalanced panel. That is, the set of hospitals is not the same for every year from 1976 to 1994 because of mergers, acquisitions, the openings and closings of hospitals during this period. The panel data technique is useful in factoring out the firm- and time-specific effects and adds robustness to the study of the effect of regulation (Baltagi, 1995). Baltagi points out that some of the advantages of using the panel data technique are that the technique: (1) controls for individual heterogeneity, (2) gives more informative data, more variability, and more efficiency during estimation, (3) is suited for studying "dynamics of adjustment," and (4) is useful for identifying and measuring effects that are not detectable from pure cross-sectional or pure time series studies (see Baltagi, 1995, pp. 3–5). With the use of panel data techniques, we need only estimate one cost function (and therefore I estimate only one set of parameters) for the entire pooled data. The random error term in the cost function is specified to contain firm- and year-specific variations making it superior to other techniques of analyzing data. For example, by analyzing the data year by year, one could obtain very different estimates of parameters for each year, thereby making the inferential process problematic. Panel data techniques do not require making simplifying assumptions regarding error disturbances such as homoscedasticity and/or absence of autocorrelation among the error terms.

The results of the analysis show that PPS did have a significant impact on the hospitals costs. I found that while all hospitals have still not achieved complete cost containment (the overt purpose of implementing PPS), the industry trend is toward cost containment. IT labor costs increased after PPS was implemented whereas IT capital costs were not affected much by its implementation. However, hospital management evidenced a change in behavior in the use of the various inputs. Furthermore, inputs such as IT capital and medical capital were not substitutes in the early years but after 1983, there is evidence of substitution between the inputs.

## 6.2 PPS AND MANAGEMENT ADJUSTMENT

The reason that the government legislated the PPS scheme of reimbursement was ostensibly cost containment. However, Broom (1988) says, "... the added costs of competition fueled by government and private sector initiatives to contain hospital costs have had unanticipated cost impacts. These include expansion and duplication of hospital services and equipment for which there is not enough need, increased hospital marketing activities, and the problem of excess beds and low hospital occupancy rates." In an attempt to empirically determine the magnitude of the effect of legislation on hospital costs, this chapter focuses on the PPS legislation.

This part of the dissertation contributes in a significant way to previous work on hospital costs and input costs in hospitals. Firstly, the use of a panel of 18 years is adequate justification for maintaining that the hospitals in the dataset are theoretically in a long-run equilibrium and that gives more credibility to the estimated cost function (Cowing et al., 1983). Previously, researchers had inadequately used cross-sectional data or small panel data such as the two-year panel data used in Vitaliano and Toren (1994) to study hospital cost functions. The goal of this research is to test the effects of regulation, and in particular the PPS method of reimbursement for Medicare patients on hospital costs and input factor use. Sloan, Morrisey and Valvona (1988) conducted an "early appraisal" of the PPS legislation effect using a data set from 1972 to 1985 for all hospitals in the nation. However, they did not specify a behavioral model. They employed simple regressions to determine the effect of the policy on hospital costs. In addition to the causality problems implicit in their methodology, drawing conclusions from their work would have been premature since only two post-PPS years were included in the data set. I include eleven post-PPS years in the dataset. While a general study of hospital costs is a fruitful endeavor, my purpose is also to relate IT and non-IT (or medical) capital costs to PPS regulation. So I analyze IT capital and non-IT (or medical) capital costs in the cost function separately whereas previous empirical work in healthcare has used only one aggregate measure for capital. The relationship between IT costs and overall costs has been analyzed in a study by Lawrence (1990). She has found that the use of innovative cost accounting systems is associated with higher capital costs. Using a case-study approach to three hospitals in New York City, Palley (1995) found that PPS reimbursement has led to a major overhauling of software and hardware of transaction processing systems in hospitals. A survey of all New York state hospitals by Palley and Conger (1995) showed that medical records processing costs increased and hospital profitability decreased due to PPS implementation.

As mentioned earlier, due to the nature of reimbursement systems prevailing during the 1976–1994 period, one may find that hospital costs increased with time in the period prior to 1983 and that they decreased with time in the periods after PPS implementation. In the overall period, the effects may diminish showing negligible change in hospital costs. If the cost of production decreases over time, the production unit is said to have undergone technical progress. On the other hand, if costs increase over time, the unit is said to have undergone technical regress (Kumbhakar 1990). Technical progress (or regress) should not be confused with technological progress (or regress) which is a reference to the state of technology. Technical progress (or regress) incorporates all types of efficiency including operational efficiency and all types of progress (or regress) including technological progress (or regress). I now state the following hypothesis on the regulation effect on progress in hospitals:

**Hypothesis 6.2.1** *Hospitals will not exhibit technical progress in the overall period. They will exhibit technical regress in the pre-PPS period but exhibit technical progress in the pot-PPS period.*

### 6.2.1 PPS and IT Use

Zimmerman (1993, p. 286) suggests that hospitals invested in sophisticated computer systems after the implementation of PPS in order to find the most suitable cost allocation structure. In addition, by 1989, hospitals began investing heavily in IT following the general trend in the economy. So we could expect to find that the technical change in hospitals led to increased demand for IT capital and labor in the post-PPS period. That is, technically put, the rate of change of share of IT costs in the total costs with respect to time would be positive in the post-PPS period. This can also be stated as technical change in hospitals was not cost-savings with respect to IT capital and labor in the post-PPS period. However, since hospitals lagged in IT implementation, we might expect that in the period prior to 1983 hospitals did not invest much in IT. In addition, prior to 1983, hospitals were acquiring more medical capital (that is, the share of medical capital in hospital cost was increasing) because by allocating those capital costs to patient care, costs were reimbursed by third-party payers. Therefore, we can expect that the rate of change of cost share of IT capital will be negative during the pre-PPS period which leads to the following hypotheses.

**Hypothesis 6.2.2** *Technical change in the industry was cost-saving with respect to IT in the pre-PPS period. Technical change was not cost-saving with respect to IT in the post-PPS period.*

In hospitals, the medical staff who govern medical decision-making and hospital administration who provide the services that physicians require to treat patients (Harris, 1977) have differing capital needs. Hospital administration would prefer to acquire IT and other capital required for administration whereas physicians would prefer to acquire medical equipment. In addition, administrators wanted to attract the best physicians to the hospitals and one way to do this was to acquire the best medical technology. Therefore, administrators were balancing the need for both IT and non-IT equipment and, in the long-run, we can reasonably assume that the demand for medical equipment will increase as output increases. However in the years since PPS implementation, particularly since physicians are recognizing the value of IT in the delivery of healthcare services, we may find that demand for IT capital will also increase with an increase in output. Since medical labor is directly related to the output level, we should see an increasing rate of change in demand for medical labor with output. The following hypotheses will be tested.

**Hypothesis 6.2.3** *The demand for IT capital will increase with an increase in the output level regardless of the period. IT labor will show a greater rate of increase in its demand with respect to output in the period after PPS implementation.*

**Hypothesis 6.2.4** *The demand for medical equipment and labor will increase with an increase in the output level regardless of the period.*

### 6.2.2 Substitution Effects between IT and other Input Factors

Next we focus on substitution and complementarity effects between the inputs. Most medical labor comprises salary of nurses and medical technicians. During the period under investigation, due to advances in medical sciences, we may expect some degree of substitution between nurses or technicians and medical capital. This will be true both before and after the PPS implementation. We may find that medical labor is a substitute for IT labor because of the change from mainframe computing to distributing computing in which data entry and validation has moved to the individual department levels, particularly in the later period. Because physicians will prefer medical equipment over IT capital, we can reasonably hypothesize that in hospitals, medical equipment is a substitute for IT capital. We therefore test the following hypotheses.

**Hypothesis 6.2.5** *Medical capital was a substitute medical labor in both periods. In the post-PPS period, medical capital was a substitute for IT capital.*

**Hypothesis 6.2.6** *Medical labor was a substitute for IT labor in the post-PPS period.*

## 6.3 TESTING THE HYPOTHESES

The hypotheses listed above can be tested if a function can be derived that relates total costs to prices of input factors and to time and output quantity. Assuming that such a function can be written in the form

$$C = C(w_1, ..., w_n, t, Y) \tag{6.1}$$

where $w_j$ are the prices of the $n$ input factors, $t$ is the time variable, and $Y$ is the output produced, we can define technical progress or regress by computing $E_t = \partial \ln C / \partial t$. If this measure is positive, it means that costs increased with time indicating technical regress whereas a negative value for the measure indicates technical progress. In order to separate pre-PPS and post-PPS measures, we estimate the mean value of $E_t$ for the data with 1983 and prior years as the pre-PPS estimate and use the data after 1983 to find the post-PPS estimate. We can test hypothesis 6.2.1 in this manner.

The total cost that appears on the left hand side in equation 6.1 is derived from the total of the costs of individual input factors. Define the share of the *j*th input factor in the total cost as $X_j$. Then, the rate of change of cost share (also the demand) with respect to time (given by equation 6.2) helps us test hypothesis 6.2.2 regarding technical change and input cost saving. That is,

$$E_{jt} = \frac{\partial \ln X_j}{\partial t}. \quad (6.2)$$

Similarly, hypotheses 6.2.3 and 6.2.4 can be tested by determining if the overall costs have increased with an increase in the output (equation 6.3). The effect of a change in the output on the cost share or demand of an input is determined by using equation 6.4. The elasticities of output are given by

$$E_Y = \frac{\partial \ln C}{\partial \ln Y}, \quad (6.3)$$

$$E_{jY} = \frac{\partial \ln X_j}{\partial \ln Y}. \quad (6.4)$$

Finally, we turn to the hypotheses regarding input substitution. Substitution between inputs can also be derived from considering the cost share of the input. If the cost share of one input increases when the price of a second input increases *ceteris paribus,* then the former input is considered a substitute for the latter input. This measure is called the Allen-Uzawa elasticity of substitution (Blackorby and Russell, 1989) and is given in equation 6.5.

$$\sigma_{jk} = \frac{1}{\partial \ln C / \partial \ln w_k} \frac{\partial \ln X_j}{\partial \ln w_k}. \quad (6.5)$$

Blackorby and Russell (1989) also define a second, more reliable measure called the Morishima elasticity of substitution given by

$$M_{jk} = \sigma_{jk} - \sigma_{jj} \quad (6.6)$$

where $\sigma_{jk}$ is the Allen-Uzawa elasticity of substitution.

The reason is that this measure is asymmetric (that is, $M_{jk} \neq M_{kj}$) due to the presence of the second term on the right hand side of equation 6.6. This second term in equation 6.6 is a measure of change in an input's cost share due to a change in its own price *ceteris paribus.* By removing the change in cost share of an input due to a change in its own price and retaining only the change in cost share of an input due to a change in the price of some other input, the resulting elasticity measure is "pure," that is, it is not confounded by other effects.

## 6.4 ECONOMETRIC MODEL

Having discussed how the hypotheses may be tested, I now turn to the problem of estimating the cost function. In general production theory, a production function (which relates the quantity of output to a set of input quantities) is estimated under a cost-minimization or profit-maximization framework as was done in the previous chapter. A complementary approach to the production function approach is to estimate the cost function (this is so because of the "duality" between the cost function and the production function formulations; see Varian, 1984). To obtain efficient and consistent estimates of the parameters of the cost function, it is jointly estimated with the cost share equations (Greene 1993, pp. 576–612). As I have already shown, the advantage of using the cost function approach is that useful measures such as the rate of technical progress, input substitution or complementarity, etc., is easily derived.

The changing regulatory environment and differences between hospitals with regard to organizational variables (such as for-profit status, teaching status, case mix ratio or severity of cases, etc.) motivate the use of panel data as opposed to pooling the data (see Zucherman, 1995, Burgess and Wilson, 1996, etc., for the importance of these variables on the organizational behavior of hospitals). I introduce firm-specific and year-specific dummy variables in the estimation of the cost function thereby factoring out possible confounds and providing more efficient and consistent estimates for the parameters of the cost function.

The cost function is specified in the translog form. The translog form is based on the second-order Taylor series approximation for any functional form and therefore is-one of the most flexible, general and versatile forms for estimating cost functions (Diewert and Wales, 1987). The translog form is well behaved and satisfies all properties required of cost functions such as the existence of second-order differentials (Varian, 1984). On the other hand, we must note that the translog function like all other parametric forms provides the best approximation of the functional form at the mean values and deviates from the actual functional form as we get further away from the mean values (Kumbhakar, 1990). In addition, the model will also suffer from specification error depending on the particular choice of inputs and outputs. The cost function $C_{it}$ for a firm $i$ in the period $t$ is written in terms of the $n$ factor prices $w_{jit}$ (where $j = 1, ...,$

$n$) as

$$\ln C_{it} = \alpha_0 + \sum_{j=1} \alpha_j \ln w_{jit} + \frac{1}{2}\sum_{j=1}\sum_{k=1} \beta_{jk} \ln w_{jit} \ln w_{kit}$$

$$+\delta_y \ln Y_{it} + \frac{1}{2}\delta_{yy}(\ln Y_{it})^2 + \sum_{j=1}^{n} \gamma_{jy} \ln w_{jit} \ln Y_{it} \quad (6.7)$$

$$+\gamma_p{}^t + \sum_{j=1}^{n} \gamma_{jp} \ln w_{jit}{}^t$$

where $Y_{it}$ is the output produced by firm $i$ in the period $t$, and $\alpha_0$, $\alpha_j$, $\beta_{jk}$, $\delta_y$, $\delta_{yy}$, $\gamma_{jy}$, $\gamma_p$ and $\gamma_{jp}$ are the parameters to be estimated.

Equation 6.7 is considered a very good approximation of any general equation that is twice differentiable (Kumbhakar, 1990). Since the cost function is general, structure is imposed on the function in the form of a restriction of homogeneity of degree one with respect to prices. Homogeneity of degree one is a necessary restriction since it ensures that when the price of an input increases by a factor, the cost function will increase proportionally if the prices of the remaining inputs are kept constant. This restriction implies that in equation 6.7 the following will hold.

$$\sum_{j=1}^{n} \alpha_j = 1,$$

$$\sum_{j=1}^{n} \beta_{jk} = 0 \quad \forall k, \quad (6.8)$$

$$\sum_{j=1}^{n} \gamma_{jy} = 0, \quad \text{and,}$$

$$\sum_{j=1}^{n} \gamma_{jp} = 0.$$

To simultaneously estimate equation 6.7 and the identifiers or restrictions 6.8 is computationally a burden. Alternatively, homogeneity of the cost function can be modeled by selecting one input factor as the "numeraire" and dividing prices of the remaining factors by the price of this factor. Then the cost function is rewritten as:

$$\ln\frac{C_{it}}{w_{1it}} = \alpha_0 + \sum_{j=2}^{n} \alpha_j \ln\frac{w_{jit}}{w_{1it}} + \frac{1}{2}\sum_{j=2}^{n}\sum_{k=2}^{n} \beta_{jk} \ln\frac{w_{jit}}{w_{1it}} \ln\frac{w_{kit}}{w_{1it}}$$

$$+\delta_y \ln Y_{it} + \frac{1}{2}\delta_{yy}(\ln Y_{it})^2 + \sum_{j=2}^{n} \gamma_{jy} \ln\frac{w_{jit}}{w_{1it}} \ln Y_{it} \quad (6.9)$$

$$+\gamma_p{}' + \sum_{j=2}^{n} \gamma_{jp} \ln\frac{w_{jit}}{w_{1it}} t + \gamma_{py} \ln Y_{it}{}' + U_{jit},$$

where $U_{jit}$ is a random disturbance term for the $j$th demand function associated with hospital $i$ in period $t$. The disturbance term captures differences in managerial ability and technical differences in production across hospitals over time. Note that the summation over the input factors in equation 6.9 starts from 2 instead of 1.

Following Kumbhakar (1990) and the panel data technique, I decompose the disturbance term $U_{jit}$ into a fixed hospital-specific error term ($\epsilon_{ji}$) and a random effect across hospitals over time ($V_{jit}$). That is, I write $U_{jit}$ as

$$U_{jit} = \epsilon_{ji} + V_{jit}. \qquad (6.10)$$

The form of equation 6.9 which includes dummy variables for individual hospitals is given by equation 6.11:

$$\ln\frac{C_{it}}{w_{1it}} = \alpha_0 + \sum_{j} \alpha_j \ln\frac{w_{jit}}{w_{1it}} + \frac{1}{2}\sum_{j}\sum_{k} \beta_{jk} \ln\frac{w_{jit}}{w_{1it}} \ln\frac{w_{kit}}{w_{1it}}$$

$$+\delta_y \ln Y_{it} + \frac{1}{2}\delta_{yy}(\ln Y_{it})^2 + \sum_{j} \gamma_{jy} \ln\frac{w_{jit}}{w_{1it}} \ln Y_{it} \quad (6.11)$$

$$+\gamma_p{}' + \sum_{j} \gamma_{jp} \ln\frac{w_{jit}}{w_{1it}} t + \gamma_{py} \ln Y_{it}{}' + \sum_{l} \delta_l D_l + U'_{jit}.$$

The input demand equations are derived using Shepard's lemma. As mentioned earlier, the total cost of production is

$$C = \sum_i w_j X_j \quad (6.12)$$

where $X_j$ is the amount of input $j$ used or demanded. We see that $C$ in equation 6.12 is a constraint that must be satisfied if the cost function formulated in equation 6.9 is applied to a cost-minimization framework. The solution is obtained by differentiating the left hand side of equation 6.9 and setting it equal to the input demand (or $X_{jit}$). The input demand equation for the $j$th factor is given by

$$X_{jit} = (\alpha_j + \beta_{jk} \ln \frac{w_{kit}}{w_{..}} + \gamma_{jy} \ln Y_{it} + \gamma_{jp}{}')(C_{it}/w_{jit}). \quad (6.13)$$

### 6.4.1 Estimation Procedure

I followed Kumbhakar and Heshmati (1993) for the steps of the estimation procedure. After the prices of inputs were calculated, the prices of IT capital, IT labor and medical labor and the total costs were divided by the price of medical equipment in order to homogenize the cost function. First, the restricted form of the cost function (6.9) and share equations (6.13) were estimated using seemingly unrelated regression. Next, the unrestricted form of the cost function (6.11) and share equations (6.13) were estimated.

The residuals obtained from the two models were used to transform the values of the prices and quantities in the cost function and share equations to reduce the heteroscedasticity in the cost function that arises from firm-specific effects. The presence of heteroscedastic error terms leads to inefficient parameter estimation (Greene, 1993). Using the transformed values of the prices and quantities, the cost function (6.9 and share equations (6.13) are jointly estimated again for the parameter values.

### 6.5 RESULTS AND DISCUSSION

Before discussing the results, we present in Table 6.1 a summary of the measures of elasticities explained in section 6.4. Table 6.2 gives the para-

**Table 6.1. Summary of measures of elasticities used to test hypotheses**

| Description | Name | Definition[1] |
|---|---|---|
| Technical progress or regress | $E_t$ | $\partial \ln C/\partial t$ |
| Elasticity of cost writ output | $E_Y$ | $\partial \ln C/\partial \ln Y$ |
| Price elasticity of cost function | $E_{jk}$ | $\partial \ln X_j/\partial \ln w_k$ |
| Elasticity of input demand wrt time | $E_{jt}$ | $\partial \ln X_j/\partial t$ |
| Elasticity of input demand wrt output | $E_{jy}$ | $\partial \ln X_j/\partial \ln Y$ |
| Allen-Uzawa elasticity of substitution | $\sigma_{jk}$ | $(c/X_j w_j)\, \partial \ln X_j/\partial \ln w_k$ |
| Morishima elasticity of substitution | $M_{jk}$ | $\partial \ln X_j/\partial \ln w_k - \partial \ln X_j/\partial \ln w_j$ |

[1] $C, t, X, Y$ and w have the same meanings as in section 6.4.

meter estimates of the cost function after the final estimation procedure. The subscript 2 for the parameters refers to IT capital, the subscript 3 to medical labor and subscript 4 to IT labor. Recall that the parameters for medical equipment will not appear because of the homogenizing procedure. These parameters can be derived from the restrictions of homogeneity given by equation 6.8.

### 6.5.1 IT Productivity Results

Before I test the hypotheses, let us turn to the issue of IT productivity. It is possible to derive the productivity contribution of input factors from the cost function even though the production function was not formulated or estimated. This is because of the duality between the cost function estimation and the production function estimation (see Varian, 1989, for the derivation, pp. 82–91). If the interaction terms between the input prices themselves and with time and output quantity is zero, then the cost function in equation 6.9 becomes a Cobb-Douglas function. I conducted an F-test between the model given by equation 6.9 and the reduced Cobb-Douglas model to test if equation 6.9 holds and found that, at a 95 percent confidence level, the null hypothesis that the interaction terms are zero was rejected, validating the form of equation 6.9. The analytical way of deriving the production function is tractable for the Cobb-Douglas function but not for the translog function. Since the Cobb-Douglas form is rejected as inadequate, I derive other measures from the cost function that proxy productivity contribution.

**Table 6.2. Estimates of the parameters of the cost function**

| Parameter | Estimate | Standard Error |
|---|---|---|
| $\alpha_0$ | −.2177 | .0225 |
| $\alpha_1$ | .9995 | .0003 |
| $\alpha_2$ | .0118 | .0019 |
| $\alpha_3$ | .0799 | .0058 |
| $\alpha_4$ | .0017 | .0002 |
| $\beta_{11}$ | −.0068 | .0011 |
| $\beta_{22}$ | −.1519 | .0096 |
| $\beta_{33}$ | .2117 | .0038 |
| $\beta_{44}$ | .0072 | .0008 |
| $\beta_{12}$ | .0039 | .0005 |
| $\beta_{13}$ | .0029 | .0009 |
| $\beta_{14}$ | −.0001 | .00006† |
| $\beta_{23}$ | .0015 | .0032† |
| $\beta_{24}$ | −.0004 | .0007† |
| $\beta_{34}$ | −.0025 | .0008 |
| $\delta_y$ | .8655 | .0548 |
| $\delta_{yy}$ | .2056 | .0422 |
| $\gamma_{1y}$ | −.0020 | .0019† |
| $\gamma_{2y}$ | −.0020 | .0087† |
| $\gamma_{3y}$ | −.0199 | .0092 |
| $\gamma_{4y}$ | −.0019 | .0007 |
| $\gamma_p$ | .1389 | .0052 |
| $\gamma_{1p}$ | .00007 | .00007† |
| $\gamma_{2p}$ | −.0122 | .0005 |
| $\gamma_{3p}$ | −.0141 | .0011 |
| $\gamma_{4p}$ | −.0002 | .00004 |
| $\gamma_{py}$ | .0019 | .0016† |

† Not significant; For all other values, $p < .001$

Productivity impacts of inputs can be determined by the estimated conditional demand function $(X_{jit})$, which is also equal to the cost elasticity of an input, $\partial \ln C / \partial \ln w_j$. The mean value of the estimate of $X_{jit}$ as given by equation 6.13 for the entire sample (1062 observations) was determined, and it was found that the standard deviation of the conditional demand estimates was too high. I extracted a subsample of 730 observations such that all values of $X_{jit}$ in the subsample were within three standard deviations from the mean values. Table 6.3 presents the means and standard deviations of the demand functions for the subsample. The productivity contribution of IT capital and labor are negative and close to zero. However, these mean values do not convey much meaning because the standard deviations are still very high indicating that even though a relatively homogeneous group of hospitals were chosen, there is much difference between "high performers" and "low performers." This further validates the methodological issue raised in the previous chapter where we contend that stochastic production frontier is a better suited econometric model because it accounts for firm-wise differences in the production function itself. The stochastic production approach yielded a very positive contribution of IT in the dataset employed. This result also serves to caution us about drawing inferences from economy-wide and sector-wide studies wherein the units of analysis are very diverse.

### 6.5.2 Discussion of Hypotheses

The estimates of the measures summarized in Table 6.1 are given in Table 6.4. The results of analysis in Table 6.4 are presented in three columns—the first column gives the results for the entire period pooled as one data set, the second column gives the results for the data before PPS regulation and the third column gives the results for the data after PPS regulation. As mentioned before, I estimate only one cost function but find the means of the measures resulting from that cost function for

**Table 6.3. Productivity estimates derived from the cost function**

| Input Factor | Productivity Estimate | Standard Deviation |
|---|---|---|
| IT Capital Input | −.00005 | .003 |
| IT Labor Input | −.00003 | .00009 |
| Non-IT Capital Input | −2.54 | 47.69 |
| Non-IT Labor Input | .00019 | .0018 |

**Table 6.4. Estimates of elasticities**

| Measure | Overall | Before PPS | After PPS |
|---|---|---|---|
| Technical progress/regress | 0.3211 | 0.4185 | 0.2514 |
| Cost Elasticity of Output | 0.3574 | 0.2974 | 0.4003 |
| Returns to Scale | 3.0918 | 3.7150 | 2.6458 |
| Price Elasticity of Medical Capital | −7.1263 | −5.1512 | −8.5398 |
| Price Elasticity of Medical Capital wrt† IT Capital | −8.4454 | 8.3733 | −20.4821 |
| Price Elasticity of Medical Capital wrt Medical Labor | −3.0574 | 8.9495 | −11.6503 |
| Price Elasticity of Medical Capital wrt IT Labor | −29.0903 | −7.1768 | −44.7731 |
| Price Elasticity of IT Capital | 1.3020 | −13.3865 | 11.8141 |
| Price Elasticity of IT Capital wrt Medical Labor | 0.0111 | −0.1003 | 0.0908 |
| Price Elasticity of IT Capital wrt IT Labor | 0.0028 | −0.0301 | 0.0264 |
| Price Elasticity of Medical Labor | −9.3355 | −32.3249 | 7.1173 |
| Price Elasticity of Medical Labor wrt IT Labor | −0.2315 | −0.8014 | 0.1765 |
| Price Elasticity of IT Labor | 60.1817 | 5.5496 | 99.2803 |
| Elasticity of Medical Capital wrt time | 0.0000 | 0.0000 | −0.0001 |
| Elasticity of IT Capital wrt time | −0.0050 | 0.0518 | −0.0457 |
| Elasticity of Medical Labor wrt time | −0.1265 | −0.4379 | 0.0964 |
| Elasticity of Medical Capital wrt time | 1.9190 | 0.1770 | 3.1658 |
| Elasticity of Medical Capital demand wrt output | 0.0010 | 0.0001 | 0.0017 |
| Elasticity of IT Capital demand wrt output | 0.1594 | −1.6390 | 1.4465 |
| Elasticity of Medical Labor demand wrt output | 3.7539 | 12.9986 | −2.8622 |
| Elasticity of IT Labor demand wrt output | −43.1443 | −3.9787 | −71.1740 |

†: stands for 'with respect to'.

the separate periods. The subscripts 1, 2, 3, and 4 stand for medical equipment, IT capital, medical labor and IT labor respectively. Each cell in Table 6.4 contains the mean value of the measure for the group.

**6.5.2.1 Hypothesis 6.2.1** The rate of technical change in the health-care industry is given by $E_t$ in Table 6.4. The positive value of $E_t$ for the overall period indicates that the overall change from 1976 to 1994 in the hospitals in the data set was technical regress. Both the pre-PPS and post-PPS periods also show technical regress separately. The second part of the hypothesis that hospitals underwent technical progress in the post-PPS period is falsified. However, there is evidence that hospitals were moving in the right direction. The fact that the pre-PPS estimates of $E_t$ are greater than the post-PPS estimates of $E_t$ means that the technical regress has slowed down in the post-PPS period and that hospital management is moving in the direction of cost containment and towards technical progress.

**6.5.2.2 Hypothesis 6.2.2** Hypothesis 2 deals with change in the industry and its relation to costs of particular inputs. We examine the values of the elasticity of input with respect to time in Table 6.4. Negative values of the measure indicate that change led to cost-savings for the input factor. We see that the change led to a decrease in IT capital costs in the overall period (elasticity of IT capital with respect to time is −0.005). However, the absolute magnitude of the change in IT costs is small. In th pre-PPS period, hospitals were increasing IT capital costs whereas in the post-PPS period, they did not increase IT capital cost share as we hypothesized. What increased costs drastically in the post-PPS period are IT labor costs. This result is credible as an average behavior because hospitals did not change hardware as a result of PPS but increased IT labor expense due to the man-hours spent on software maintenance as a result of PPS (see Palley and Conger, 1995). We also see that medical capital expense remained relatively constant due to PPS. However the rate of change of medical labor cost share increased in the post-PPS period indicating the medical labor-expending nature of that period.

**6.5.2.3 Hypothesis 6.2.3 and 6.2.4** The elasticity of the cost function with respect to output in Table 6.4 measures the magnitude and direction of the change in total costs for a unit change in output. The value of 0.3574 indicates that costs did not increase proportionately with output level. The values for pre- and post-PPS are not very different indicating that the relationship between output and costs did not change much due to PPS. The returns to scale measure (RTS) can be derived by taking the inverse of the output elasticity of the cost function (see Table 6.4). A value of RTS greater than 1 indicates that the presence of increasing returns to scale. This leads to the conclusion that mergers of hospitals will produce gain in production efficiency. In the post-DRG period, I find that there has been a decrease in the RTS measure. This leads to the interpretation that hospitals will probably not find it more efficient to merge operations in the PPS era rather than prior to PPS. This conflicts with the current trend in the healthcare industry where we find that multihospital systems (MHSs) have been growing at a fast rate in the US since PPS implementation (Sloan, Morrisey, and Valvona, 1992). This conflict may be due to the fact that the unit of analysis in our study is a hospital (and not an MHS). The returns to scale measure at this level cannot then be easily extended to the formation of MHSs. Further extending this reasoning, it is also possible that since the cost function here uses only one output (patient-days) whereas hospital mergers may be engendered by other considerations other than increase in patient-days, the estimation did not capture the advantages of forming MHSs. For example, the formation of MHSs lead to an increase in volume of output. That is, MHSs can generate more revenues yet keep fixed costs low. Prior to PPS, under the cost-based reimbursement scheme, the cost structure of hospitals had higher fixed costs because all costs were reimbursed.

I examine the elasticity of input factors with respect to output as an incidental result from the analysis. We can see that when the output increased, in the pre-PPS period hospitals did not increase IT capital expense and in the post-PPS period they tended to increase IT capital expense. Another finding is that the medical labor decreased with output in the post-PPS period. I conclude that in the later period, hospitals had become more efficient with respect to medical labor and in spite of increases in the output, did not increase medical labor expense.

**6.5.2.4 Hypothesis 6.2.5 and 6.2.6** Substitution between input factors occurs due to the sensitivity of demand of one input factor to prices of other factors. These effects can be measured using the Allen-Uzawa elasticity of substitution or the Morishima elasticity of substitution. The main difference between the two is that the Morishima measure is asymmetric (input substitution between 1 and 2 is not the same as input substitution between 2 and 1) and preserves Hicksian properties of the model (Blackorby and Russell, 1989). The Allen-Uzawa measure ($\sigma_{jk}$) and the

**Table 6.5. Estimates of elasticities of substitution**

| Measure | Overall | Before PPS | After PPS |
|---|---|---|---|
| $\sigma_{12}$ | −3.9658 | −24.5206 | 10.7447 |
| $\sigma_{13}$ | −2.7692 | 0.9414 | −5.4248 |
| $\sigma_{14}$ | 4.2346 | 1.3023 | 6.3332 |
| $\sigma_{23}$ | 0.0306 | 0.1894 | −0.0830 |
| $\sigma_{24}$ | 0.0088 | 0.0542 | −0.0238 |
| $\sigma_{34}$ | 0.1573 | −0.0535 | 0.3082 |
| $M_{12}$ | 337.8293 | −63.0907 | 624.7560 |
| $M_{21}$ | −3.9590 | −24.5138 | 10.7514 |
| $M_{13}$ | −2.7625 | 0.9482 | −5.4181 |
| $M_{31}$ | −5.3527 | 1.8197 | −10.4858 |
| $M_{14}$ | 15.8393 | 4.8712 | 23.6889 |
| $M_{41}$ | 4.2414 | 1.3091 | 6.3399 |
| $M_{23}$ | −2.5529 | 1.0677 | −5.1440 |
| $M_{32}$ | 341.8258 | −38.3807 | 613.9283 |
| $M_{24}$ | 11.6135 | 3.6231 | 17.3320 |
| $M_{42}$ | 341.8039 | −38.5159 | 613.9876 |
| $M_{34}$ | 11.7621 | 3.5154 | 17.6640 |
| $M_{43}$ | −2.4262 | 0.8248 | −4.7528 |

Morishima measure ($M_{jk}$) are also given in Table 6.5. Positive value of $\sigma_{jk}$ indicate that $j$ and $k$ inputs are substitutes. The values of $\sigma_{12}$ in Table 6.5 indicates that in the pre-PPS period, IT capital (input 2) and medical capital (input 1) were not substitutes. However, after PPS implementation, the two input factors have become substitutes. Similarly, the measures $\sigma_{23}$ and $\sigma_{24}$ are negative in the pre-PPS period and positive in the post-PPS period. This means that IT capital became substitutes with both medical labor and IT labor after PPS implementation. Medical labor and capital were substitutes prior to PPS and are no longer substitutes since PPS (see $\sigma_{13}$ in the table). Medical labor and IT labor ($\sigma_{34}$) were not substitutes prior to 1983 and became substitutes in the later period. This coincides with the move to distributed computing in which departments took over the data entry and some processing responsibilities from the IT departments. On examining the Morishima elasticities, we obtain similar results. Substitution between input factors is indicated by negative values. IT capital is found to be substituted with the remaining three input factors prior to PPS but not after PPS implementation.

# CHAPTER 7

# Non-Parametric Productivity Analysis

## 7.1 INTRODUCTION

The results from the parametric techniques in the previous chapters should be interpreted keeping in mind the statistical assumptions underlying the formulations. The choice of the functional form, the structure and form of error terms etc., all contribute to specification error while using parametric techniques (Varian, 1984). Alternatively, production efficiency can also be determined by relying on linear programming techniques without having to specify a functional form for the production function hence called non-parametric techniques (Charnes et al., 1978, 1994; Banker et al., 1984; Färe et al., 1994). The nonparametric technique, which is explained in greater detail in the following sections, requires only one assumption—the production set is convex. By tightly enveloping the output set from above and the input set from below, the production frontier can be determined from the subset of firms that used least inputs to generate maximum outputs. Since the data is thus "enveloped," this technique has been called Data Envelopment Analysis or DEA by management scientists; see Banker et al. (1984), Seiford (1996), etc. In the following section, I first describe the nonparametric approach and then present the theoretical and practical contributions from this work.

## 7.2 NONPARAMETRIC APPROACH TO PRODUCTION

As mentioned above, in the nonparametric approach to analyzing production efficiency, the production function is not specified in a functional form. Instead, the data on the input quantities used and the output quantities produced for a sample of firms is used in order to determine the production possibility set. Figure 7.1 illustrates the concept. Consider an industry in which firms use two inputs $X$ and $Z$ in order to produce output $U$. Let point $R$ represent the choice of inputs for a firm in the input quantity space. If several firms can be represented in this space, then the production frontier shown by the convex envelope $Y$ can be derived for the set of firms using linear programming techniques (for simplicity, the figure shows the envelope assuming constant returns to scale of production and strong disposability of inputs; see, for example, Färe et al. 1994, pp. 32–44, for a discussion on returns to scale and disposability of inputs). Obviously, firms that are closer to the frontier are more efficient than firms that are further away from it. The technical efficiency of a firm is given by *OS/OR,* which is the proportion by which input quantities can be radially (and feasibly) reduced. If the price ratio between inputs $X$ and $Z$ is given by the iso-cost line *PQ,* then by operating at the point $S$, the firm has chosen a technically efficient input mix which, however, is not allocatively efficient. This is because the costs will be higher at S than at E, and by using less of Z and more of X (i.e., by moving from S to E), the

**Figure 7.1. Illustration of technical and allocative efficiency**

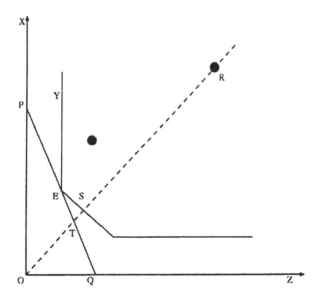

firm can produce the same output in a technically efficient fashion but also at a lower cost.

The ratio OT/OS is called the firm-specific allocative efficiency (hereafter FAE) of the firm which measures the proportion by which the cost in a technically efficient input mix is higher than the minimum feasible cost of production. Note that this measure does not capture how far from S point E is. This deviation from E to S is probably due to the fact that managers are perceiving a different set of prices or shadow prices for the inputs rather than the real prices and are equating the ratio of the marginal products to the ratio of the shadow prices (Eakin and Kniesner, 1988). The deviation of the ratio of the shadow prices from the ratio of the real prices (which is also equal to the ratio of the marginal products of inputs) is called input-specific allocative inefficiency (hereafter IAE).

If the marginal products of the inputs were known, then the IAE can be easily calculated as done in Chapter 5. While the marginal products can be derived in the parametric technique by differentiating the production function, marginal products cannot be determined in the nonparametric technique at points such as E because the envelope is not differentiable at this point. In this chapter, I show how the marginal products of inputs and therefore the IAE can be empirically estimated in the nonparametric case. This way we not only find IAE of inputs with respect to IT but also extend the existing theory on parametric and nonparametric techniques by comparing the two techniques using IAE and FAE which has not yet been done.

There are pros and cons of using either technique (parametric or nonparametric) for productivity analysis. The major differences center around error from noisy data and specification error (Lovell, 1992, p. 19). Parametric techniques attempt to model noise in the data whereas nonparametric techniques combine noise and inefficiency. On the other hand, parametric techniques could suffer from specification error which is not a problem in nonparametric techniques. Nonparametric techniques place weight on outlier observations whereas parametric techniques estimate average behavior and discard outliers (Charnes et al 1994, pg. 9).

The differences in the two techniques and the results from the two techniques and their implications for managers and policymakers make the exercise of comparing the two techniques fruitful. Among the first to compare the two techniques is the Banker et al. (1986) paper which showed that DEA performs better when the underlying production technology has variable returns to scale whereas the translog production function analysis may lead to acceptance of the constant returns to scale null hypothesis since the estimation is based on *average* behavior. They stress the need for more comparative studies between the two techniques. Using rank correlations between technical efficiency ratings between the DEA formulation and deterministic Cobb-Douglas formulation for real data, Bjurek et al. (1990) found that the correlations were high ($\geq 0.83$) and were particular high ($\geq 0.95$) for values of returns to scale close to 1. Gong and Sickles (1992) used simulated panel data to show that for simple underlying technologies, stochastic production frontiers performed better than DEA if the functional forms used for the production frontier were close to the actual production function. Otherwise DEA performed better. In all of the above comparative papers, allocative efficiency seems to be a maintained hypothesis. In this chapter, I extend the comparison literature on the two techniques by comparing the allocative efficiency measures resulting from the two techniques.

In order to maintain continuity and comparability with the previous chapters, I model the hospital inputs as IT and non-IT labor and capital, and the output as adjusted patient days.

## 7.3 THEORETICAL FORMULATIONS OF NONPARAMETRIC MODELS

Before deriving the allocative efficiency, we first define the various measures such as technical and cost efficiency. The pioneering definitions of technical efficiency of production by Koopmans (1951), Debreu (1951), and Farrell (1957) have been extrapolated to define other measures of efficiency of firms such as cost efficiency, allocative efficiency, etc. Cost efficiency is determined by calculating the minimum feasible cost of production and comparing it to the actual costs. Let the input mix used by a firm $j$ be given by $\mathbf{x}^j$. The prices of the inputs faced by the firm are given by the vector $\mathbf{p}^j$. If $\mathbf{x}^j_0$ is the minimum cost input quantities required to produce the same output level, then cost efficiency *C.E.* is defined as

$$C.E. = \frac{\mathbf{p}^j \cdot \mathbf{x}^j_o}{\mathbf{p}^j \cdot \mathbf{x}^j}. \quad (7.1)$$

The minimum cost input quantities $\mathbf{x}_{jo}$ for the firm $j$ is the solution obtained by solving the following linear programming problem for the firm.

$$min \qquad \mathbf{p}^j \cdot \mathbf{x}^j$$

$$\mathbf{x}^j, \lambda$$

$$s.t. \ \mathbf{Y} \cdot \lambda \geq \mathbf{y}^j \tag{7.2}$$

$$\mathbf{X} \cdot \lambda \leq \mathbf{x}^j$$

$$\lambda \geq \mathbf{0}.$$

In the above equations, the uppercase variables are matrices containing data for all firms. That is, $\mathbf{Y}$ is a $m \times n$ matrix containing data for $n$ firms and $m$ outputs, $\mathbf{X}$ is a $k \times n$ matrix containing data for $n$ firms and $k$ inputs and, $\lambda$ and $\mathbf{O}$ are $1 \times n$ matrices of weights and zeroes, respectively. The lowercase variables represent data in vector form for a firm $j$.

The same prices, input and output quantities used in the previous chapters are used here. The results of the cost efficiency is presented in Tables (7.1–7.2) and in Tables 7.3–7.4 by year for each firm for the entire sample. We did not pool the data over the years. Instead the cost efficiency and technical efficiency measures were separately determined for each year. Tables 7.1 and 7.2 contain the allocative values from 1976 to 1985. Tables 7.3 and 7.4 contain the allocative efficiency values from 1986 to 1994. The hospitals are identified by an identification number. For each year, only one hospital is cost efficient ($C.E. = 1$).

Technical efficiency (based on the Debreu-Farrell radial efficiency measure) is independent of prices of inputs and measures the radial distance of the firm from the "best practices" frontier in the input quantity space. This measure $\theta$ can be obtained by solving the following linear programming problem

$$min \ \theta$$

$$\theta, \lambda$$

$$s.t. \ \mathbf{Y} \cdot \lambda \geq \mathbf{y}^j \tag{7.3}$$

$$\mathbf{X} \cdot \lambda \leq \mathbf{x}^j \theta$$

$$\lambda \geq \mathbf{0}.$$

In DEA literature, the above LP problem is rewritten (e.g., Charnes et al., 1994, p. 37) as

$$min \ \theta - \epsilon .1 s^+ - \epsilon .1 s^-$$

$$\theta, \lambda s^+, s^-$$

$$s.t. \ \mathbf{Y} \cdot \lambda - s^+ - \mathbf{y}^j = 0 \tag{7.4}$$

$$\mathbf{x}^j \cdot \theta - \mathbf{X} \cdot \lambda - s^- = 0.$$

**Table 7.1. Allocative efficiency values for hospitals from 1976 to 1985**

| Hosp | 1976 | 1977 | 1978 | 1979 | 1980 | 1981 | 1982 | 1983 | 1984 | 1985 |
|------|------|------|------|------|------|------|------|------|------|------|
| 7 | 0.84 | 0.79 | 0.56 | NA | NA | NA | NA | NA | NA | NA |
| 14 | 0.70 | 0.64 | 0.52 | NA | 0.54 | 0.57 | 0.59 | 0.55 | 0.61 | 0.72 |
| 22 | NA | 0.90 | 0.83 | 0.81 | 0.87 | 0.92 | 1.00 | 0.97 | 0.87 | 0.79 |
| 26 | 0.78 | 0.79 | 0.76 | 0.82 | 0.79 | 1.00 | 0.97 | 0.88 | 0.65 | 0.72 |
| 27 | 0.60 | 0.58 | 0.52 | 0.60 | 0.64 | 0.78 | 0.75 | 0.70 | 0.67 | 0.73 |
| 32 | 0.71 | 0.71 | 0.65 | 0.72 | 0.11 | 0.15 | 0.20 | 0.22 | 0.27 | 0.30 |
| 35 | NA | NA | NA | NA | NA | NA | NA | NA | NA | NA |
| 36 | 0.72 | 0.76 | 0.71 | 0.73 | 0.79 | 0.92 | 0.96 | 0.73 | 0.60 | 0.65 |
| 38 | 0.69 | 0.70 | 0.69 | 0.77 | 0.82 | 0.88 | 0.89 | 0.86 | 0.66 | 0.69 |
| 39 | 0.64 | 0.60 | 0.61 | 0.69 | 0.65 | 0.82 | 0.93 | 0.79 | 0.86 | 0.94 |
| 43 | NA | NA | NA | NA | NA | 0.69 | 0.74 | 0.78 | 0.85 | 0.77 |
| 46 | 0.41 | 0.30 | 0.27 | 0.27 | 0.33 | 0.32 | 0.38 | 0.41 | 0.42 | 0.38 |
| 47 | 0.77 | 0.75 | 0.66 | 0.70 | 0.71 | 0.90 | 0.74 | 0.64 | 0.56 | 0.61 |
| 50 | 0.70 | 0.64 | 0.61 | 0.68 | 0.70 | 0.85 | 0.91 | 0.91 | 0.70 | 0.54 |
| 58 | 0.89 | 0.91 | 0.67 | 0.71 | 0.76 | 0.90 | 0.88 | 0.72 | 0.68 | 0.77 |
| 63 | NA | 0.77 | 0.74 | 0.80 | 0.88 | 0.92 | 0.96 | 0.96 | 0.77 | 0.91 |
| 73 | NA | 0.69 | 0.60 | 0.72 | 0.79 | 0.92 | 0.93 | 0.66 | 0.73 | 0.63 |
| 78 | NA | NA | NA | 0.57 | 0.51 | 0.63 | 0.65 | 0.68 | 0.64 | 0.64 |
| 81 | 0.81 | 0.79 | 0.69 | 0.77 | 0.77 | 0.99 | 0.90 | 0.72 | 0.66 | 0.92 |
| 84 | 0.45 | 0.47 | 0.50 | 0.56 | 0.60 | 0.80 | 0.82 | 0.60 | 0.64 | 0.65 |
| 85 | NA | NA | NA | NA | NA | NA | NA | NA | NA | 0.64 |
| 92 | NA | NA | NA | NA | NA | NA | 0.97 | 0.95 | 0.91 | 0.79 |
| 102 | 0.67 | 0.60 | 0.59 | 0.68 | 0.74 | 0.88 | 0.94 | 0.79 | 0.84 | 0.79 |
| 104 | NA | NA | 0.44 | 0.58 | 0.58 | 0.67 | 0.84 | 0.66 | 0.59 | 0.62 |
| 106 | NA | NA | NA | NA | NA | NA | NA | NA | NA | 0.68 |
| 125 | NA | 0.46 | 0.47 | 0.45 | 0.59 | 0.50 | 0.55 | 0.50 | NA | NA |
| 126 | 0.46 | 0.46 | 0.52 | 0.60 | 0.70 | 0.78 | 0.85 | 0.78 | 0.83 | 0.67 |
| 130 | 0.83 | 0.85 | 0.88 | 0.89 | 0.89 | 0.99 | 0.82 | 0.64 | 0.48 | 0.49 |

**Table 7.2. Allocative efficiency values for hospitals from 1976 to 1985 (Contd.)**

| Hosp | 1976 | 1977 | 1978 | 1979 | 1980 | 1981 | 1982 | 1983 | 1984 | 1985 |
|------|------|------|------|------|------|------|------|------|------|------|
| 131 | 0.79 | 0.81 | 0.45 | 0.50 | 0.52 | 0.69 | 0.67 | 0.64 | 0.68 | 0.78 |
| 132 | 0.36 | 0.37 | 0.43 | 0.49 | 0.53 | 0.65 | 0.56 | 0.56 | 0.57 | 0.59 |
| 134 | 0.59 | 0.45 | 0.45 | 0.47 | 0.56 | 0.58 | 0.70 | 0.61 | 0.67 | 0.82 |
| 138 | 0.67 | 0.68 | 0.53 | 0.58 | 0.61 | 0.71 | 0.68 | 0.62 | 0.71 | 0.70 |
| 139 | 0.55 | 0.58 | 0.61 | 0.66 | 0.69 | 0.89 | 0.94 | 0.91 | NA | 0.91 |
| 142 | 0.91 | 0.85 | 0.84 | 0.85 | 0.76 | 0.90 | 0.99 | 0.99 | 1.00 | 0.91 |
| 143 | 0.62 | 0.63 | 0.68 | 0.71 | 0.78 | 0.91 | 0.96 | 0.85 | 0.56 | 0.57 |
| 145 | 0.62 | 0.57 | 0.49 | 0.56 | 0.59 | 0.70 | 0.64 | 0.62 | 0.61 | 0.72 |
| 146 | 0.41 | 0.48 | 0.43 | NA | 0.53 | 0.88 | 0.94 | 1.00 | 0.99 | 0.92 |
| 148 | 0.50 | 0.52 | 0.57 | 0.65 | 0.69 | 0.68 | 0.75 | 0.66 | 0.51 | 0.46 |
| 151 | 0.62 | 0.66 | 0.56 | 0.59 | 0.60 | 0.78 | 0.83 | 0.72 | 0.80 | 0.69 |
| 156 | NA | 0.47 | 0.45 | 0.55 | 0.62 | 0.61 | 0.74 | 0.53 | 0.49 | 0.52 |
| 157 | 0.46 | 0.46 | 0.46 | 0.48 | 0.55 | 0.76 | 0.86 | 0.71 | 0.66 | 0.64 |
| 159 | 0.69 | 0.74 | 0.57 | 0.59 | 0.60 | 0.73 | 0.75 | 0.70 | 0.71 | 0.61 |
| 161 | NA | NA | NA | 0.73 | 0.80 | 0.95 | 0.94 | 0.63 | 0.60 | 0.63 |
| 164 | 0.66 | 0.71 | 0.71 | 0.76 | 0.78 | 0.92 | 0.83 | 0.71 | 0.70 | 0.81 |
| 168 | 0.65 | 0.66 | 0.70 | 0.65 | 0.67 | 0.85 | 0.90 | 0.85 | 0.83 | 0.68 |
| 171 | 0.72 | 0.82 | 0.79 | 0.82 | 0.84 | 0.95 | 0.97 | 0.76 | 0.75 | 0.82 |
| 175 | 0.81 | 0.55 | 0.50 | NA | NA | 0.58 | 0.74 | 0.61 | 0.65 | 0.66 |
| 180 | NA | NA | NA | NA | NA | NA | 0.85 | 0.85 | 0.65 | 0.49 |
| 182 | 0.36 | 0.39 | 0.40 | 0.42 | 0.46 | 0.60 | 0.73 | 0.67 | 0.63 | 1.00 |
| 183 | NA | 0.82 | 0.74 | 0.80 | 0.85 | NA | NA | 0.67 | 0.66 | 0.85 |
| 184 | 1.00 | 1.00 | 1.00 | 1.00 | 1.00 | NA | NA | 0.74 | 0.80 | 0.89 |
| 185 | 0.77 | 0.78 | 0.76 | 0.83 | 0.85 | NA | NA | 0.61 | 0.78 | 0.81 |
| 188 | NA | 0.59 | 0.61 | 0.73 | 0.73 | 0.82 | 0.82 | NA | NA | 0.62 |
| 189 | 0.80 | 0.73 | 0.60 | 0.63 | 0.65 | 0.52 | 0.50 | 0.48 | 0.65 | 0.83 |
| 191 | 0.60 | 0.71 | 0.73 | 0.75 | 0.76 | 0.81 | 0.99 | 0.85 | 0.91 | 0.91 |
| 192 | 0.50 | 0.59 | 0.54 | 0.65 | 0.66 | 0.59 | 0.68 | 0.64 | 0.71 | 0.84 |
| 197 | NA | NA | NA | NA | NA | NA | NA | NA | NA | 0.27 |

**Table 7.3. Allocative efficiency values for hospitals from 1986 to 1994**

| Hosp | 1986 | 1987 | 1988 | 1989 | 1990 | 1991 | 1992 | 1993 | 1994 |
|------|------|------|------|------|------|------|------|------|------|
| 7 | NA | NA | NA | NA | NA | NA | NA | NA | NA |
| 14 | 0.77 | 0.67 | 0.66 | 0.70 | 0.58 | 0.99 | 0.92 | 0.47 | 0.36 |
| 22 | 0.80 | 0.48 | 0.63 | 0.58 | 0.57 | 0.92 | 0.69 | 0.70 | 0.55 |
| 26 | 0.76 | 0.62 | 0.71 | 0.78 | 0.82 | 0.99 | 0.98 | 0.67 | 0.67 |
| 27 | 0.60 | 0.52 | 0.57 | 0.62 | 0.73 | 0.83 | 0.86 | 0.66 | 0.54 |
| 32 | 0.34 | 0.45 | 0.60 | 0.71 | 0.86 | 0.72 | 0.72 | 0.55 | 0.51 |
| 35 | 0.51 | 0.55 | 0.68 | 0.40 | 0.39 | 0.76 | 0.69 | 0.29 | 0.34 |
| 36 | 0.53 | 0.50 | 0.64 | 0.79 | 0.81 | 0.99 | 0.97 | NA | NA |
| 38 | 0.68 | 0.58 | 0.63 | 0.63 | 0.68 | 0.97 | 0.95 | 0.49 | 0.45 |
| 39 | 0.75 | 0.60 | 0.60 | 0.60 | 0.64 | 0.81 | 0.65 | 0.58 | 0.61 |
| 43 | 0.71 | 0.57 | 0.73 | 0.65 | 0.61 | 0.77 | 0.66 | 0.58 | 0.46 |
| 46 | 0.42 | 0.47 | 0.52 | 0.57 | 0.58 | 0.50 | 0.40 | 0.31 | 0.26 |
| 47 | 0.68 | 0.60 | 0.55 | NA | NA | NA | NA | NA | NA |
| 50 | 0.60 | 0.60 | 0.72 | 0.73 | 0.78 | 0.89 | 0.87 | 0.68 | 0.58 |
| 58 | 0.76 | 0.70 | 0.64 | 0.64 | 0.62 | 0.89 | 0.79 | 0.55 | 0.46 |
| 63 | 1.00 | 0.66 | 0.80 | 0.91 | 1.00 | 0.72 | 0.62 | 0.75 | 0.84 |
| 73 | 0.69 | 0.53 | 0.57 | 0.66 | 0.60 | 0.83 | 0.79 | 0.77 | 0.66 |
| 78 | 0.63 | 0.48 | 0.57 | 0.53 | 0.52 | 0.63 | 0.72 | 0.47 | 0.45 |
| 81 | 0.93 | 0.87 | 1.00 | 1.00 | 0.89 | 0.73 | 0.62 | 0.77 | 0.79 |
| 84 | 0.60 | 0.53 | 0.56 | 0.61 | 0.62 | 1.00 | 0.99 | 0.64 | 0.59 |
| 85 | 0.61 | 0.49 | 0.44 | 0.34 | 0.40 | NA | NA | NA | NA |
| 92 | 0.58 | 0.51 | 0.59 | NA | NA | 0.82 | 0.79 | NA | NA |
| 102 | 0.72 | 0.54 | 0.71 | 0.76 | 0.87 | 0.96 | 0.97 | 0.71 | 0.52 |
| 104 | 0.52 | 0.42 | 0.54 | 0.53 | 0.62 | 0.91 | 0.90 | 0.26 | 0.27 |
| 106 | 0.59 | 0.42 | 0.47 | 0.50 | 0.55 | 0.76 | 0.78 | 0.44 | 0.54 |
| 125 | NA | NA | NA | NA | NA | NA | NA | NA | NA |
| 126 | 0.59 | 0.54 | 0.63 | 0.64 | 0.61 | 0.81 | 0.86 | 0.49 | 0.44 |
| 130 | 0.55 | 0.50 | 0.57 | 0.60 | 0.72 | 0.94 | 0.94 | 0.66 | 0.47 |

**Table 7.4. Allocative efficiency values for hospitals from 1986 to 1994 (Contd.)**

| Hosp | 1986 | 1987 | 1988 | 1989 | 1990 | 1991 | 1992 | 1993 | 1994 |
|------|------|------|------|------|------|------|------|------|------|
| 131 | 0.82 | 0.61 | 0.61 | 0.60 | 0.64 | 1.00 | 1.00 | 0.49 | 0.42 |
| 132 | 0.58 | 0.40 | 0.49 | 0.57 | NA | 0.76 | 0.69 | 0.79 | 0.75 |
| 134 | 0.53 | 0.43 | 0.54 | 0.54 | 0.58 | 0.86 | 0.78 | 0.47 | 0.47 |
| 138 | 0.74 | 0.63 | 0.81 | 0.85 | 0.89 | 0.83 | 0.78 | 0.73 | 0.60 |
| 139 | 0.89 | 0.81 | 0.93 | 0.93 | 0.93 | 0.83 | 0.80 | 0.87 | 1.00 |
| 142 | 0.95 | 0.79 | 0.91 | 0.90 | 0.91 | 0.97 | 0.97 | 0.68 | 0.69 |
| 143 | 0.53 | 0.51 | 0.63 | 0.64 | NA | NA | NA | NA | NA |
| 145 | 0.34 | 0.26 | 0.33 | 0.47 | 0.66 | 0.89 | 0.88 | 0.56 | 0.52 |
| 146 | 0.94 | 0.67 | 0.76 | 0.76 | 0.58 | 0.99 | 0.98 | 0.58 | 0.65 |
| 148 | 0.35 | NA | 0.37 | NA | NA | NA | NA | NA | NA |
| 151 | NA | NA | NA | NA | NA | NA | NA | NA | NA |
| 156 | 0.54 | 0.49 | 0.59 | 0.55 | 0.55 | 0.92 | 0.84 | 0.39 | 0.50 |
| 157 | 0.69 | 0.74 | 0.70 | 0.56 | 0.76 | 0.61 | 0.67 | NA | NA |
| 159 | 0.50 | 0.51 | 0.59 | 0.68 | 0.74 | 0.80 | 0.87 | 0.71 | 0.59 |
| 161 | 0.59 | 0.42 | 0.51 | 0.49 | 0.53 | 0.86 | 0.85 | 0.38 | 0.42 |
| 164 | 0.76 | 0.59 | 0.69 | 0.80 | 0.68 | 0.99 | 0.98 | 0.55 | 0.46 |
| 168 | 0.63 | 0.51 | 0.58 | 0.61 | 0.68 | 0.97 | 1.00 | 0.60 | 0.52 |
| 171 | 0.89 | 0.76 | 0.80 | 0.80 | 0.67 | 0.83 | 0.81 | 0.66 | 0.67 |
| 175 | 0.86 | 0.64 | 0.70 | 0.63 | 0.62 | 0.90 | 0.86 | 0.55 | 0.50 |
| 180 | 0.62 | 0.46 | 0.55 | 0.58 | 0.60 | 0.78 | 0.81 | 0.53 | 0.56 |
| 182 | 1.00 | 1.00 | 0.90 | 0.86 | 0.85 | 1.00 | 1.00 | 1.00 | NA |
| 183 | 0.79 | 0.53 | 0.59 | 0.76 | 0.77 | 0.93 | 0.82 | 0.82 | 0.64 |
| 184 | 0.96 | NA | NA | NA | NA | NA | NA | NA | NA |
| 185 | 0.65 | 0.49 | NA | NA | NA | NA | NA | NA | NA |
| 188 | 0.62 | 0.53 | NA | NA | NA | NA | NA | NA | NA |
| 189 | 0.50 | 0.49 | 0.45 | NA | NA | NA | NA | NA | NA |
| 191 | 0.81 | 0.64 | 0.74 | 0.78 | 0.84 | 0.70 | 0.61 | 0.74 | 0.64 |
| 192 | 0.51 | NA | NA | NA | NA | NA | NA | NA | NA |
| 197 | 0.31 | 0.28 | 0.42 | 0.42 | 0.60 | 0.92 | 0.80 | 0.70 | 0.59 |

The variables $s^+$ and $s^-$ represent output and input slacks, respectively. $\in$ is a constant, infinitesimal non-Archimedean number. To avoid numerical problems due to the choice of $\in$ in standard mathematical programming software, the LP is solved in two stages (e.g., Charnes et al., 1994, p. 32). First, optimal $\theta$ is determined and in the second stage the slack variables are determined. The results of the technical efficiency is presented by year for each firm in Tables 7.5–7.8. We see that more firms are technically efficient than cost efficient. In addition, it also seems that firms are consistently either high or low performers over the years.

The firm-specific allocative efficiency (FAE) can now be calculated from the estimates of cost efficiency and technical efficiency as

$$\text{FAE} = \frac{C.E.}{\theta}. \quad (7.5)$$

FAE does not tell us what the inefficiency in allocation is in the selection of each input quantity. It only gives an overall allocative inefficiency measure for the firm which is not very informative beside telling us by how much the cost function could have been lower. If we were interested in the inefficiency in the allocation of IT with respect to other input factors, IAE gives an estimation of the measure. However, before going into IAE calculations, in the next section I present the derivation of the FAE for the parametric case so that the FAEs from both techniques can be compared. In particular, for the parametric case, we rely on the stochastic production frontier results.

## 7.4 FIRM-SPECIFIC ALLOCATIVE INEFFICIENCY

Firm-specific allocative inefficiency is given by equation 7.5. Substituting equation 7.1 for C.E. yields

$$\text{FAE} = \frac{\mathbf{p}^j \cdot \mathbf{x}_o^{\,j}}{\theta \mathbf{p}^j \cdot \mathbf{x}^j}. \quad (7.6)$$

For the Cobb-Douglas production function, the factor quantities are related by the first order conditions given by equation (5.4) in chapter 5.

**Table 7.5. Technical efficiency values for hospitals from 1976 to 1986**

| Hosp | 1976 | 1977 | 1978 | 1979 | 1980 | 1981 | 1982 | 1983 | 1984 | 1985 |
|------|------|------|------|------|------|------|------|------|------|------|
| 7 | 0.70 | 0.64 | 0.59 | NA | NA | NA | NA | NA | NA | NA |
| 14 | 0.50 | 0.43 | 0.40 | NA | 0.50 | 0.54 | 0.54 | 0.55 | 0.57 | 0.58 |
| 22 | NA | 0.93 | 0.75 | 0.75 | 0.89 | 1.00 | 1.00 | 1.00 | 0.85 | 0.71 |
| 26 | 0.86 | 0.77 | 0.73 | 0.75 | 0.85 | 1.00 | 0.99 | 0.99 | 0.99 | 0.90 |
| 27 | 0.74 | 0.78 | 0.73 | 0.77 | 0.79 | 0.83 | 0.87 | 0.86 | 0.85 | 0.88 |
| 32 | 0.85 | 0.74 | 0.72 | 0.82 | 0.87 | 0.88 | 0.84 | 0.86 | 0.90 | 0.86 |
| 35 | NA | NA | NA | NA | NA | NA | NA | NA | NA | NA |
| 36 | 0.82 | 0.72 | 0.69 | 0.75 | 0.86 | 0.88 | 0.88 | 0.85 | 0.89 | 0.86 |
| 38 | 0.82 | 0.75 | 0.70 | 0.82 | 0.86 | 0.95 | 0.95 | 0.92 | 0.84 | 0.84 |
| 39 | 0.97 | 0.95 | 0.77 | 0.76 | 0.90 | 1.00 | 0.89 | 0.98 | 1.00 | 1.00 |
| 43 | NA | NA | NA | NA | NA | 1.00 | 0.99 | 0.77 | 0.73 | 0.89 |
| 46 | 1.00 | 1.00 | 1.00 | 1.00 | 1.00 | 1.00 | 0.94 | 0.88 | 0.87 | 0.84 |
| 47 | 0.83 | 0.76 | 0.70 | 0.78 | 0.81 | 0.80 | 0.81 | 0.80 | 0.77 | 0.76 |
| 50 | 0.71 | 0.68 | 0.65 | 0.76 | 0.80 | 0.88 | 0.90 | 0.83 | 0.83 | 0.81 |
| 58 | 0.87 | 0.68 | 0.68 | 0.85 | 0.88 | 0.92 | 0.89 | 0.91 | 0.96 | 0.99 |
| 63 | NA | 0.89 | 0.69 | 0.84 | 0.91 | 0.96 | 0.96 | 0.82 | 0.80 | 1.00 |
| 73 | NA | 1.00 | 1.00 | 1.00 | 1.00 | 1.00 | 1.00 | 1.00 | 1.00 | 1.00 |
| 78 | NA | NA | NA | 1.00 | 1.00 | 1.00 | 0.77 | 0.76 | 0.74 | 0.93 |
| 81 | 0.97 | 0.85 | 0.76 | 0.82 | 1.00 | 1.00 | 0.89 | 0.86 | 0.84 | 0.91 |
| 84 | 0.74 | 0.66 | 0.66 | 0.75 | 0.80 | 0.78 | 0.79 | 0.70 | 0.75 | 0.74 |
| 85 | NA | NA | NA | NA | NA | NA | NA | NA | NA | 0.81 |
| 92 | NA | NA | NA | NA | NA | NA | 1.00 | 1.00 | 1.00 | 1.00 |
| 102 | 0.94 | 0.73 | 0.69 | 0.76 | 0.80 | 0.84 | 0.88 | 0.82 | 0.94 | 0.89 |
| 104 | NA | NA | 0.84 | 0.75 | 0.87 | 1.00 | 0.77 | 0.70 | 0.82 | 0.78 |
| 106 | NA | NA | NA | NA | NA | NA | NA | NA | NA | 1.00 |
| 125 | NA | 1.00 | 1.00 | 1.00 | 1.00 | 1.00 | 1.00 | 1.00 | NA | NA |
| 126 | 0.80 | 0.77 | 0.71 | 0.77 | 0.84 | 0.95 | 0.92 | 1.00 | 1.00 | 0.89 |
| 130 | 0.82 | 0.75 | 0.71 | 0.80 | 1.00 | 0.98 | 0.95 | 0.85 | 0.73 | 0.74 |

**Table 7.6. Technical efficiency values for hospitals from 1976 to 1986 (Contd.)**

| Hosp | 1976 | 1977 | 1978 | 1979 | 1980 | 1981 | 1982 | 1983 | 1984 | 1985 |
|------|------|------|------|------|------|------|------|------|------|------|
| 131 | 0.95 | 0.78 | 0.76 | 0.86 | 0.99 | 0.95 | 0.90 | 0.85 | 0.89 | 0.87 |
| 132 | 0.77 | 0.75 | 0.71 | 0.77 | 0.78 | 0.85 | 0.86 | 0.84 | 0.78 | 0.76 |
| 134 | 1.00 | 1.00 | 0.84 | 0.86 | 0.79 | 0.88 | 0.82 | 0.83 | 0.82 | 0.81 |
| 138 | 0.87 | 0.81 | 0.76 | 0.87 | 0.94 | 0.92 | 0.95 | 0.91 | 0.92 | 0.88 |
| 139 | 0.83 | 0.74 | 0.67 | 0.81 | 0.89 | 0.95 | 1.00 | 0.99 | NA | 0.98 |
| 142 | 0.89 | 0.77 | 0.74 | 0.81 | 0.88 | 0.96 | 1.00 | 1.00 | 1.00 | 0.97 |
| 143 | 0.82 | 0.76 | 0.72 | 0.83 | 0.87 | 1.00 | 0.92 | 0.90 | 0.85 | 0.86 |
| 145 | 1.00 | 0.71 | 0.65 | 0.72 | 0.83 | 0.86 | 0.88 | 0.89 | 0.91 | 0.87 |
| 146 | 0.90 | 0.90 | 0.75 | NA | 0.99 | 1.00 | 1.00 | 1.00 | 1.00 | 0.84 |
| 148 | 0.77 | 0.72 | 0.72 | 0.77 | 0.76 | 0.84 | 0.74 | 0.67 | 0.61 | 0.66 |
| 151 | 0.58 | 0.52 | 0.52 | 0.70 | 0.79 | 0.80 | 0.89 | 0.88 | 0.80 | 0.64 |
| 156 | NA | 1.00 | 1.00 | 1.00 | 1.00 | 0.86 | 0.87 | 0.84 | 0.76 | 0.72 |
| 157 | 0.70 | 0.59 | 0.53 | 0.58 | 0.62 | 0.79 | 0.77 | 0.72 | 0.67 | 0.60 |
| 159 | 0.78 | 0.68 | 0.63 | 0.71 | 0.72 | 0.79 | 0.82 | 0.86 | 0.92 | 0.95 |
| 161 | NA | NA | NA | 0.89 | 0.86 | 0.93 | 0.89 | 0.86 | 0.81 | 0.87 |
| 164 | 0.79 | 0.66 | 0.65 | 0.77 | 0.81 | 0.83 | 0.86 | 0.87 | 0.92 | 0.97 |
| 168 | 0.74 | 0.67 | 0.70 | 0.78 | 0.86 | 0.95 | 0.92 | 0.93 | 0.94 | 0.84 |
| 171 | 0.97 | 0.82 | 0.74 | 0.82 | 0.89 | 0.95 | 0.93 | 0.92 | 0.94 | 0.97 |
| 175 | 0.78 | 0.69 | 0.60 | NA | NA | 0.80 | 0.78 | 0.74 | 0.76 | 0.61 |
| 180 | NA | NA | NA | NA | NA | NA | 1.00 | 1.00 | 1.00 | 1.00 |
| 182 | 0.92 | 0.74 | 0.75 | 0.80 | 0.89 | 0.95 | 0.98 | 1.00 | 1.00 | 1.00 |
| 183 | NA | 0.92 | 0.72 | 0.86 | 0.89 | NA | NA | 0.90 | 0.89 | 0.92 |
| 184 | 1.00 | 1.00 | 1.00 | 1.00 | 1.00 | NA | NA | 1.00 | 1.00 | 1.00 |
| 185 | 0.84 | 0.81 | 0.81 | 0.90 | 0.98 | NA | NA | 0.83 | 0.84 | 0.81 |
| 188 | NA | 0.82 | 0.76 | 0.80 | 0.86 | 0.92 | 0.94 | NA | NA | 0.90 |
| 189 | 0.76 | 0.80 | 0.84 | 0.85 | 0.92 | 0.91 | 0.78 | 0.86 | 1.00 | 0.99 |
| 191 | 1.00 | 0.88 | 0.76 | 0.77 | 0.83 | 0.97 | 0.93 | 0.85 | 0.88 | 0.76 |
| 192 | 0.92 | 0.81 | 0.86 | 0.81 | 0.88 | 0.94 | 0.78 | 0.76 | 0.76 | 0.89 |
| 197 | NA | NA | NA | NA | NA | NA | NA | NA | NA | 0.56 |

**Table 7.7. Technical efficiency values for hospitals from
1987 to 1994**

| Hosp | 1986 | 1987 | 1988 | 1989 | 1990 | 1991 | 1992 | 1993 | 1994 |
|------|------|------|------|------|------|------|------|------|------|
| 7 | NA | NA | NA | NA | NA | NA | NA | NA | NA |
| 14 | 0.59 | 0.57 | 0.62 | 0.48 | 0.57 | 0.53 | 0.57 | 0.48 | 0.61 |
| 22 | 0.73 | 0.80 | 0.83 | 0.85 | 0.75 | 0.62 | 0.72 | 0.54 | 0.83 |
| 26 | 0.83 | 0.84 | 0.87 | 0.75 | 0.80 | 0.77 | 0.74 | 0.71 | 0.95 |
| 27 | 0.84 | 0.95 | 1.00 | 0.89 | 0.89 | 0.91 | 0.82 | 0.77 | 0.80 |
| 32 | 0.80 | 0.78 | 0.91 | 0.85 | 0.90 | 0.69 | 0.89 | 0.86 | 1.00 |
| 35 | 0.94 | 1.00 | 1.00 | 1.00 | 1.00 | 0.88 | 0.96 | 0.99 | 1.00 |
| 36 | 0.86 | 0.89 | 1.00 | 1.00 | 0.85 | 0.84 | 0.45 | NA | NA |
| 38 | 0.74 | 0.84 | 0.86 | 0.88 | 0.91 | 0.77 | 0.82 | 0.74 | 0.91 |
| 39 | 1.00 | 1.00 | 1.00 | 0.92 | 0.90 | 0.78 | 1.00 | 0.95 | 0.92 |
| 43 | 0.92 | 0.81 | 0.74 | 0.92 | 0.88 | 0.88 | 1.00 | 1.00 | 1.00 |
| 46 | 1.00 | 1.00 | 1.00 | 1.00 | 1.00 | 1.00 | 1.00 | 1.00 | 1.00 |
| 47 | 0.86 | 0.79 | 0.55 | NA | NA | NA | NA | NA | NA |
| 50 | 0.80 | 0.93 | 0.89 | 0.93 | 0.83 | 0.80 | 0.82 | 0.73 | 0.81 |
| 58 | 0.90 | 0.90 | 0.93 | 0.90 | 0.93 | 0.79 | 0.94 | 0.66 | 0.85 |
| 63 | 1.00 | 1.00 | 1.00 | 1.00 | 1.00 | 1.00 | 1.00 | 1.00 | 1.00 |
| 73 | 1.00 | 1.00 | 1.00 | 1.00 | 1.00 | 0.85 | 0.83 | 0.61 | 0.67 |
| 78 | 0.82 | 0.94 | 1.00 | 1.00 | 1.00 | 1.00 | 0.88 | 0.80 | 0.90 |
| 81 | 1.00 | 1.00 | 1.00 | 1.00 | 0.96 | 0.96 | 1.00 | 0.81 | 0.95 |
| 84 | 0.70 | 0.74 | 0.78 | 0.68 | 0.75 | 0.59 | 0.54 | 0.49 | 0.59 |
| 85 | 1.00 | 1.00 | 1.00 | 1.00 | 1.00 | NA | NA | NA | NA |
| 92 | 1.00 | 1.00 | 1.00 | NA | NA | 1.00 | 1.00 | NA | NA |
| 102 | 0.83 | 0.78 | 0.89 | 0.95 | 0.81 | 0.75 | 0.74 | 0.66 | 0.86 |
| 104 | 1.00 | 0.96 | 0.91 | 0.87 | 0.84 | 0.69 | 0.72 | 1.00 | 1.00 |
| 106 | 1.00 | 1.00 | 0.95 | 1.00 | 1.00 | 0.90 | 0.83 | 0.93 | 1.00 |
| 125 | NA | NA | NA | NA | NA | NA | NA | NA | NA |
| 126 | 0.90 | 1.00 | 1.00 | 1.00 | 1.00 | 1.00 | 0.85 | 0.88 | 0.86 |
| 130 | 0.74 | 0.83 | 0.79 | 0.81 | 0.73 | 0.69 | 0.63 | 0.57 | 0.79 |

**Table 7.8. Technical efficiency values for hospitals from 1987 to 1994(Contd.)**

| Hosp | 1986 | 1987 | 1988 | 1989 | 1990 | 1991 | 1992 | 1993 | 1994 |
|------|------|------|------|------|------|------|------|------|------|
| 131 | 0.84 | 0.81 | 0.84 | 0.75 | 0.75 | 0.66 | 0.61 | 0.55 | 0.69 |
| 132 | 0.65 | 1.00 | 1.00 | 0.91 | NA | 0.83 | 1.00 | 0.86 | 1.00 |
| 134 | 0.84 | 0.85 | 0.83 | 0.92 | 0.92 | 0.78 | 0.77 | 0.81 | 0.87 |
| 138 | 0.88 | 0.89 | 0.92 | 0.89 | 0.93 | 0.97 | 1.00 | 0.69 | 0.89 |
| 139 | 1.00 | 0.97 | 0.89 | 0.89 | 1.00 | 0.94 | 0.93 | 1.00 | 1.00 |
| 142 | 0.89 | 1.00 | 0.90 | 0.92 | 0.96 | 0.82 | 0.77 | 0.66 | 0.85 |
| 143 | 0.85 | 0.92 | 0.98 | 0.89 | NA | NA | NA | NA | NA |
| 145 | 0.91 | 0.80 | 0.76 | 0.84 | 0.89 | 0.80 | 0.74 | 0.64 | 0.72 |
| 146 | 1.00 | 0.88 | 0.97 | 1.00 | 0.80 | 0.80 | 0.80 | 0.74 | 1.00 |
| 148 | 0.93 | NA | 1.00 | NA | NA | NA | NA | NA | NA |
| 151 | NA | NA | NA | NA | NA | NA | NA | NA | NA |
| 156 | 0.68 | 0.69 | 0.62 | 0.71 | 0.67 | 0.55 | 0.65 | 0.76 | 0.76 |
| 157 | 0.56 | 0.63 | 0.72 | 0.64 | 0.84 | 1.00 | 0.77 | NA | NA |
| 159 | 0.85 | 0.84 | 0.83 | 0.81 | 0.74 | 0.52 | 0.61 | 0.55 | 0.64 |
| 161 | 0.84 | 0.46 | 0.79 | 0.77 | 0.79 | 0.69 | 0.66 | 0.69 | 0.79 |
| 164 | 0.87 | 0.89 | 0.88 | 0.76 | 0.78 | 0.69 | 0.64 | 0.59 | 0.70 |
| 168 | 0.88 | 0.81 | 0.91 | 0.87 | 0.87 | 0.82 | 0.75 | 0.69 | 0.89 |
| 171 | 0.87 | 0.87 | 0.90 | 0.85 | 0.83 | 0.80 | 0.85 | 0.62 | 0.80 |
| 175 | 0.61 | 0.58 | 0.66 | 0.66 | 0.68 | 0.71 | 0.765 | 0.73 | 0.77 |
| 180 | 0.81 | 0.87 | 1.00 | 1.00 | 1.00 | 1.00 | 1.00 | 1.00 | 1.00 |
| 182 | 1.00 | 1.00 | 1.00 | 1.00 | 1.00 | 1.00 | 1.00 | 1.00 | NA |
| 183 | 0.86 | 0.93 | 1.00 | 1.00 | 1.00 | 1.00 | 1.00 | 0.83 | 0.95 |
| 184 | 1.00 | NA | NA | NA | NA | NA | NA | NA | NA |
| 185 | 0.71 | 0.83 | NA | NA | NA | NA | NA | NA | NA |
| 188 | 0.87 | 0.85 | NA | NA | NA | NA | NA | NA | NA |
| 189 | 1.00 | 1.00 | 0.86 | NA | NA | NA | NA | NA | NA |
| 191 | 0.73 | 1.00 | 0.80 | 1.00 | 1.00 | 1.00 | 1.00 | 0.88 | 1.00 |
| 192 | 0.75 | NA | NA | NA | NA | NA | NA | NA | NA |
| 197 | 0.79 | 0.97 | 1.00 | 1.00 | 0.94 | 0.82 | 0.85 | 0.70 | 0.92 |

The ratio of the marginal products will equal the price ratio for the efficient input mix $x^j_o$ whereas in the inefficient case, the price ratio will deviate from the ratio of the marginal products by a factor of IAE.

If we assume that the production function is Cobb-Douglas as given in Chapter 5, then, for an allocatively efficient input mix, $x^j_o$ ($\forall j \neq 1$) can be written in terms of $x^1_o$

$$x^j_o = \frac{a_j P_1}{a_1 P_j} x^1_o, \quad (7.7)$$

and for an allocatively inefficient mix that is technically efficient, we can write,

$$x^j = \frac{a_j P_1}{a_1 P_j} x^1 e^{-u_1}. \quad (7.8)$$

$$\text{FAE} = \frac{x^1}{x^1_o} \frac{1}{\theta} \frac{\sum_1^k a^j}{a_1 + \sum_2^k a^j \cdot e^{(j-1)}}. \quad (7.9)$$

$x^1_o$, the *argmin* of the cost function, is calculated as a function of output, prices and parameters given in 7.10.

$$x^1_o = \left[ \frac{y}{a_o} \sum_2^k \left( \frac{a_1 P_j}{a_j P_1} \right)^{a_j} \right] \sum_1^k a_j. \quad (7.10)$$

The point estimates of FAE calculated from equation (7.9) for the parametric estimation are used to determine the relative ranking of the firms. These rankings are correlated with the rankings obtained from the nonparametric estimation (as has been in literature; eg., Gong and Sickles 1992). The rank correlation is given in Table 7.9. The parametric and nonparametric results for FAE show high correlation for the years 1976 to 1982. Thereafter the correlations are lower. Indeed after 1990, the correlation is negative. These results may be explained based on the returns to scale of production that may have been affected by the policy changes in 1983 (the introduction of prospective payment system for Medicare patients) and in 1989.

In the next section, we derive the input-specific allocative efficiency for the non-parametric case and explore the relation between the rankings yielded by the parametric and non-parametric techniques based on IAE.

## 7.5 INPUT-SPECIFIC ALLOCATIVE EFFICIENCY

The usefulness of allocative inefficiency lies in determining over- or underuse of individual inputs with respect to their prices and thereby finding the feasible minimum cost input mix. Literature on determining allocative inefficiency using nonparametric techniques does not address the of IAE. I propose a way to determine the IAE after the technically efficient production frontier has been identified. I correlate the ranking of the firms based on IAE with the ranking of the firms based on FAE for the nonparametric case. In addition, I also correlate the rankings of the IAEs from the nonparametric case with those of the parametric case.

In order to estimate the IAE for the nonparametric case, I followed these steps. First, I find the set of all points on the technically efficient frontier by solving 7.3 for θ. By radially reducing the input quantities by θ and subtracting the slack, I obtain the technically efficient input mix. Alternatively, the weighted sum of inputs and outputs for all firms will also yield the same quantity (Ali and Seiford, 1990). The points given by he weighted values of inputs and outputs represent the frontier. The graph of these points are fit to a model given by equation 7.11.

$$\ln y = a_o + \sum_{j=1}^{4} a_j \ln x_j. \tag{7.11}$$

Formally, following Färe et al. (1994), the graph of the technology (*GR*) is the collection of all feasible input–output vectors. That is,

$$GR = (x,y) \in \Re^{k+m}_+ : y \in P(x), x \in \Re^k_+$$

$$= (x,y) \in \Re^{k+m}_+ : x \in L(y), y \in \Re^m_+ \tag{7.12}$$

twhere $P(x)$ is the output correspondence and $L(y)$ is the input correspondence. $x$, $y$, $k$ and $m$ have the same meaning as before. Since *GR* is convex,

$$\mathbf{X}^j \lambda \in L(y) \ \forall j = 1, ..., k, \text{ and}$$

$$\mathbf{Y}^j \lambda \in P(x) \ \forall j = 1, ..., m. \tag{7.13}$$

**Table 7.9. Correlation between FAE rankings for parametric and non-parametric techniques**

| Year | Correlation value | p-value |
|------|-------------------|---------|
| 1976 | 0.830 | .0001 |
| 1977 | 0.929 | .0001 |
| 1978 | 0.897 | .0001 |
| 1980 | 0.902 | .0001 |
| 1981 | 0.839 | .0001 |
| 1982 | 0.817 | .0001 |
| 1983 | 0.813 | .0001 |
| 1984 | 0.664 | .0001 |
| 1985 | 0.533 | .0001 |
| 1986 | 0.609 | .0001 |
| 1987 | 0.597 | .0001 |
| 1988 | 0.617 | .0001 |
| 1989 | 0.644 | .0001 |
| 1990 | 0.581 | .0001 |
| 1991 | −0.365 | .014 |
| 1992 | −0.440 | .003 |
| 1993 | 0.451 | .0001 |
| 1994 | 0.466 | .0022 |

We consider only the technically efficient firms in order to locate the locus of the frontier, that is, firms for which $\theta$ equals 1. As a radial measure,

$$\theta x^j \in Isoq\, L(y) \tag{7.14}$$

where *Isoq* refers to isoquant (same output). Under the assumption of strong disposability of inputs,

$$W\, Eff\, L(y) = Isoq\, L(y) \tag{7.15}$$

**Table 7.10. Estimates of the coefficients of the production frontier**

| Year | $\ln(a_0)$ | $a_1$ | $a_2$ | $a_3$ | $a_4$ |
|------|-----------|-------|-------|-------|-------|
| 1976 | 6.40 (.23) | 0.75 (.04) | −0.04 (.01) | 0.32 (.04) | −0.006(.004)* |
| 1977 | 4.61 (.21) | 1.03 (.02) | 0.07 (.03) | −0.04 (.02) | −0.07 (.02) |
| 1978 | 6.57 (.18) | 1.12 (.02) | −0.23 (.03) | 0.04 (.02) | 0.07 (.01) |
| 1979 | 5.93 (.16) | 1.12 (.02) | −0.18 (.02) | 0.01 (.02)* | 0.06 (.02) |
| 1980 | 6.03 (.22) | 1.09 (.02) | −0.11 (.03) | 0.01 (.02)* | −0.02 (.02)* |
| 1981 | 5.08 (.36) | 1.09 (.24) | −0.09 (.03) | 0.05 (.02) | 0.03 (.02)* |
| 1982 | 5.16 (.36) | 1.11 (.03) | −0.11 (.03) | −0.002 (.01)* | 0.04 (.01) |
| 1983 | 4.80 (.19) | 1.05 (.04) | −0.056(.02) | 0.028 (.02)* | −0.027(.01) |
| 1984 | 4.06 (.18) | 0.837(.02) | 0.072(.02) | 0.096 (.01) | 0.01 (.01)* |
| 1985 | 4.88 (.31) | 0.91 (.04) | −0.034 (.03)* | 0.118 (.02) | 0.036(.01) |
| 1986 | 6.01 (.55) | 1.07 (.06) | −0.08 (.05)* | 0.14 (.04) | −0.06 (.02) |
| 1987 | 3.68 (.65) | 0.97 (.07) | 0.01 (.04)* | 0.10 (.05) | 0.05 (.02) |
| 1988 | 3.43 (.42) | 0.93 (.06) | 0.04 (.03)* | 0.12 (.05) | 0.04 (.03)* |
| 1989 | 2.90 (.49) | 0.94 (.05) | 0.04 (.04)* | 0.142 (.04) | 0.069(.03) |
| 1990 | 2.47 (.52) | 0.93 (.05) | 0.08 (.04) | 0.09 (.02) | 0.06 (.03) |
| 1991 | 0.62 (.58)* | 0.73 (.07) | 0.22 (.05) | 0.05 (.04)* | 0.11 (.03) |
| 1992 | −0.18 (.98)* | 0.89 (.11) | 0.26 (.07) | −0.03 (.09)* | 0.06 (.04)* |
| 1993 | 4.53(1.78) | 1.63 (.13) | −0.34 (.11) | −0.44 (.11) | 0.22 (.09) |
| 1994 | 3.37 (.91) | 1.15 (.08) | 0.01 (.07)* | 0.02 (.07)* | −0.01 (.04)* |

* Estimate not significant.

which formally proves that the input sets of these technically efficient firms form the Weakly Efficient input Correspondence or *W Eff L(y)* which along with *P(x)* gives the production frontier.

The production frontier is estimated using the points given by the technically efficient firms. Table (7.10) presents the results of the estimation. The large *t*-values indicate overfitting which is expected in this case. In addition, the curve seems high elastic to the non-IT labor and relatively inelastic to the remaining inputs for most years.

The slopes of the production frontier with respect to each input factor give the marginal products of the input factors. The IAE is then de-

**Table 7.11. Correlation between parametric and nonparametric IAE rankings**

| Year | $IAE_1$ | $IAE_2$ | $IAE_3$ |
|------|---------|---------|---------|
| 1976 | 0.13 (.40) | 0.38 (.01) | 0.46 (.003) |
| 1977 | −0.11 (.46) | 0.65 (.0001) | −0.29 (.04) |
| 1978 | −0.03 (.85) | 0.61 (.0001) | −0.33 (.02) |
| 1979 | −0.01 (.94) | 0.48 (.0007) | −0.41 (.004) |
| 1980 | −0.23 (.11) | 0.44 (.002) | −0.28 (.04) |
| 1981 | 0.29 (.04) | 0.98 (.0001) | 0.60 (.0001) |
| 1982 | −0.02 (.85) | 0.88 (.0001) | 0.39 (.005) |
| 1983 | 0.16 (.27) | 0.91 (.0001) | 0.36 (.009) |
| 1984 | 0.26 (.07) | 0.91 (.0001) | 0.64 (.0001) |
| 1985 | 0.15 (.26) | 0.94 (.0001) | 0.49 (.0002) |
| 1986 | −0.10 (.45) | 0.91 (.0001) | 0.28 (.04) |
| 1987 | 0.14 (.31) | 0.86 (.0001) | 0.86 (.0001) |
| 1988 | 0.49 (.0003) | 0.92 (.0001) | 0.73 (.0001) |
| 1989 | 0.41 (.005) | 0.98 (.0001) | 0.98 (.0001) |
| 1990 | 0.62 (.0001) | 0.93 (.0001) | 0.49 (.0006) |
| 1991 | 0.23 (.12) | 0.71 (.0001) | 0.54 (.0001) |
| 1992 | 0.22 (.13) | 0.85 (.0001) | 0.26 (.09) |
| 1993 | 0.05 (.74) | 0.71 (.0001) | −0.09 (.57) |
| 1994 | 0.09 (.54) | 0.96 (.0001) | 0.36 (.02) |

termined by comparing the ratio of marginal products for a pair of inputs to the ratio of their prices. Non-IT labor is taken as the reference factor. Then the IAE for each input with respect to non-IT labor is used to rank the firms. I correlate these rankings with the IAE rankings obtained from the stochastic production function estimation in Chapter 5 (see Table 7.11). Note that $IAE_2$ rankings are highly correlated between the two techniques. The initial years do not show very significant correlation between the techniques probably due to data errors. However, as seen in Table 7.9, the FAE are highly correlated between the two techniques. This leads us to ask whether the IAEs derived are correlated to the FAE

**Table 7.12. Correlation between IAE and FAE rankings for non-parametric case**

| Year | $IAE_1$ | $IAE_2$ | $IAE_3$ |
|------|---------|---------|---------|
| 1976 | 0.02 (.89) | 0.02 (.89) | 0.41 (.007) |
| 1977 | −0.32 (.03) | 0.21 (.15) | −0.17 (.24) |
| 1978 | −0.20 (.17) | 0.17 (.22) | −0.12 (.42) |
| 1979 | −0.17 (.23) | 0.38 (.007) | −0.17 (.25) |
| 1980 | −0.31 (.03) | 0.42 (.002) | −0.27 (.06) |
| 1981 | −0.17 (.26) | 0.11 (.47) | 0.24 (.10) |
| 1982 | −0.67 (.0001) | −0.07 (.62) | −0.32 (.02) |
| 1983 | −0.53 (.0001) | −0.20 (.15) | −0.18 (.21) |
| 1984 | −0.57 (.0001) | 0.02 (.84) | 0.05 (.73) |
| 1985 | −0.53 (.0001) | −0.08 (.56) | −0.45 (.0006) |
| 1986 | −0.48 (.0002) | −0.25 (.07) | −0.14 (.29) |
| 1987 | 0.09 (.51) | −0.14 (.31) | −0.16 (.25) |
| 1988 | 0.12 (.42) | −0.19 (.18) | −0.02 (.90) |
| 1989 | −0.10 (.48) | −0.07 (.62) | 0.02 (.85) |
| 1990 | 0.05 (.75) | 0.05 (.74) | −0.19 (.19) |
| 1991 | 0.34 (.02) | −0.32 (.03) | −0.11 (.46) |
| 1992 | 0.20 (.17) | −0.006(.97) | 0.26 (.09) |
| 1993 | −0.41 (.007) | 0.006(.97) | −0.60 (.0001) |
| 1994 | −0.18 (.25) | 0.10 (.53) | −0.18 (.25) |

for the non-parametric technique. That is, is IAE any indicator of FAE? Table 7.12 contains the correlation of IAE rankings with the FAE rankings both obtained from the nonparametric formulation. For most of the values, the correlation is not significant. The only significant pattern is that $IAE_2$ seems consistently highly correlated with FAE for most years. So it would seem that not all IAEs are indicators of FAE. The reason probably lies in the price elasticity and the absolute prices of the input factors. Since the price ranges of non-IT labor and IT labor are much closer than the price ranges of non-IT labor with the other inputs, it might have greater effect on IAE. On the other hand, price elasticity of an input factor is high, it may have a bigger effect on the FAE than an input factor with lower price elasticity. While the results in Table (7.9) somewhat validate our estimation procedure of IAE in the nonparametric case, the use of simulated data might yield more conclusive results.

CHAPTER 8
# Conclusions

## 8.1 SUMMARY OF RESEARCH PURPOSE

In this study I analyzed the productivity of IT in the healthcare industry in the face of regulation and organizational choices. I used parametric and nonparametric techniques to investigate the productivity question of IT and other hospital inputs. Both a production function approach and a cost function approach is employed in the parametric investigation. The use of various approaches can lead to triangulation and better understanding of the results. Chapter 5 contained the formulations and results from using the production function, first assuming away any inefficiencies and then by incorporating inefficiencies as explanatory parameters in the production formulations. The former technique is called the deterministic production approach and the latter is called the stochastic production approach. By expressing the production behavior in terms of costs in the cost function approach delineated in Chapter 6, I look at productivity of IT and several other issues pertaining to regulation. The cost function approach does not incorporate allocative inefficiency in the formulation. As opposed to the parametric technique, nonparametric techniques do not require specifying a functional form for the production function. Instead, the input and output quantities are used to determine the production set using linear programming techniques. The nonparametric technique formulation and the results are explained in Chapter 7.

The following sections summarize the results from the earlier chapters. In addition to pointing out the limitations of each technique, I also present directions for future research.

## 8.2 PRODUCTION FUNCTION APPROACH

Overall, the production function approach resulted in the evidence of positive contribution of IT to the production of healthcare services. The issue of the quality of capital which is particularly relevant to IT is resolved to show that quality adjustments to investment can cause dramatic differences in productivity results. The results from the stochastic production approach showed that firms vary greatly in the efficiency of production processes and resource allocations and that this variation does indeed lead to differences in results in ex ante productivity calculations.

One limitation of the production function approach as given in Chapter 5 is the assumption of cost minimization behavior for hospitals for all years from 1976 to 1994. Prior to 1983, hospitals did not have the incentive to reduce costs, rather most hospitals were attempting to maximize charges to third-party payers. Therefore, other models such as revenue maximization could be applied in the years 1976 to 1983. The problem with this approach, however, would be the difficulty of estimating one production function by specifying different behavioral models for the two time periods. A second limitation relates to the calculation of input price for non-IT capital all of which was assumed to be medical technology. The prices for plant and supplies were not factored in because the data on plant and supplies was not available. Third, even though deflators and dummy variables were used to account for time variation in data, there are bound to be fixed and random time-related effects for each firm. In such a case, the use of panel data techniques is recommended (Baltagi, 1995; Skinner, 1994). Fourth, even though there is precedence in literature regarding the use of a single output model for hospitals (e.g., Newhouse, 1994), the aggregation of inpatient and outpatient output measures into a single measure can be a limitation of empirical studies. One of the reasons for this limitation is that the hospital is a multiple-output producing unit and may be working to optimize several objectives. Finally, the use of accounting data that was reported to a regulatory agency may have led to erroneous conclusions. As mentioned earlier, hospitals resorted to clever cost allocation procedures before and after PPS implementation and so the resulting capital stock and labor cost allocation could have been noisy (see, for example, Eldenburg and Kallapur, 1996 for how costs were allocated to outpatients after PPS implementation). It is difficult to say how the results will be affected if the data were devoid of manipulations due to cost allocations.

## 8.3 COSTS OF PRODUCTION, IT AND REGULATION

The cost function approach used in Chapter 6 complements the production function approach in Chapter 5. The added advantage of the cost function approach is that it is possible to determine the effect of regulation on hospital costs and on other hospital management issues. The cost function was formulated using the same inputs and outputs as in Chapter 5 and followed a specification conducive to panel data analysis. The focus of regulation was the PPS reimbursement scheme legislated in 1983.

The results showed that the management of hospital costs differed greatly between the pre-PPS and post-PPS periods. The PPS legislation led to a lower level of technical regress in hospitals meaning that hospitals were moving toward cost containment. I find that IT was a substitute for other input factors in the post-PPS period. I fail to find a statistically significant contribution from IT investments to the production of services in yielded positive returns to hospitals.

## 8.4 NONPARAMETRIC ANALYSIS

Using nonparametric analysis, I try to avoid model specification problems that arise in parametric analyses. In order to triangulate the results from the stochastic parametric analysis, allocative inefficiencies are determined in the nonparametric case both for the hospital and for each individual input factor.

## 8.5 FUTURE WORK

It would be useful, as Weill (1992) has done, to determine the productivity impacts of the different types of information systems such as executive information systems, strategic information systems, transaction-processing systems, etc. At the very least, even the separation of data processing and data communication impacts can be studied. For example, the growth of multihospital systems and the need for health information networks has led to increased investment in data communication in the past years. Therefore, by further disaggregating data as data processing and data communications, productivity gains can be compartmentalized as coordination gains and productivity gains.

Osterman (1990) says that the multiplicative fashion in which technology enters the production function may be simplistic. Senior managers expend considerable time and energy on capital investments, but not on the human resource and organizational requirements of introducing and maintaining/using the technology. Future research must consider more appropriate technology models while assessing IT productivity.

# Appendix A

List of Accounts in Hospitals by category.
1. Category: Inpatient Accounts
   - Intensive Care Unit
   - Coronary Care
   - Semi-intensive and Intermediate Care
   - Acute Care
   - Psychiatric Care
   - Alcoholism Treatment Center
   - Nursery
   - Skilled Nursing Facility
   - Hospice
   - Other Daily Hospital Services
2. Category: Ancillary Accounts
   - Labor and Delivery
   - Surgical Services
   - Recovery Room
   - Anesthesia
   - Central Services
   - IV Therapy
   - Laboratory (including Blood Bank)
   - Electrodiagnosis
   - Magnetic Resonance Imaging
   - CT Scanning Service
   - Radiology—Diagnostic
   - Radiology—Therapeutic

- Nuclear Medicine
- Pharmacy
- Respiratory Therapy
- Dialysis
- Physical Therapy
- Other Physical Medicine
- Occupational Therapy
- Speech Therapy
- Recreational Therapy
- Electromyography
- Psychiatric Day Care
- Emergency Room
- Ambulance
- Short Stay
- Clinics
- Free Standing Clinical Services
- Air Transportation
- Home Health Therapy
- Lithotripsy
- Organ Acquisition
- Other Ancillary Services

3. Category: Non-revenue Accounts
- Research
- Research and Education
- Nursing Education
- Licensed Practical Nurse Program
- Medical Postgraduate Education
- Paramedical Education
- Student Housing
- Other Educational Activities
- Printing and Duplicating
- Dietary
- Cafeteria
- Laundry and Linen
- Social Services
- Central Transportation
- Employee Housing
- Purchasing
- Plant
- Housekeeping

- Other General Services
- Accounting of Total Fiscal Services
- Communications
- Patient Accounts
- Data Processing
- Admitting
- Other Fiscal Services
- Hospital Administration
- Public Relations
- Management Engineering
- Personnel
- Auxiliary Groups
- Chaplaincy Services
- Medical Library
- Medical Records
- Medical Staff
- Health Care Renew
- Nursing Administration
- Nursing Float Personnel
- Inservice—Nursing
- Inservice Education—Other
- Other Administrative Services

# References

[1]  Alpar, P., and M. Kim, "A Microeconomic Approach to the Measurement of Information Technology Value," *Journal of Management Information Systems,* vol. 7, no. 2, Fall 1990, pp. 55–69.

[2]  Andrianos, J., and M. Dykan, "Using Cost Accounting Data to Improve Clinical Value," *Healthcare Financial Management,* May 1996, pp. 44–48.

[3]  Baily, M.N., and R.J. Gordon. "The Productivity Slowdown, Measurement Issues, and the Explosion of Computer Power," *Brookings Papers on Economic Activity,* vol. 2, 1988, pp. 347–420.

[4]  Baltagi, Badi H. *Econometric Analysis of Panel Data,* Macmillan Publishing, London, England, 1995.

[5]  Banker, R.D., A. Charnes, and W.W. Cooper, "Some Models for Estimating Technical and Scale Inefficiencies in Data Envelopment Analysis," *Management Science,* vol. 30, no. 9, September 1984, pp. 1078–1092.

[6]  Banker, R.D., R.F. Conrad, and R.J. Strauss, "A Comparative Application of Data Envelopment Analysis and Translog Methods: An Illustration of Hospital Production," *Management Science,* vol. 32, No. 1, January 1986, pp. 30–44.

[7]  Bell, G., F. Chesnais, and H. Wienart, "Highlights of the Proceedings," *Technology and Productivity: A Challenge for Economic Policy,* Organization for Economic Co-operation and Development Publications, Paris, 1991.

[8]  Berndt, E.R., and C.J. Morrison, "High-Tech Capital Formation and Economic Performance in US Manufacturing Industries: An Exploratory Analysis," *Journal of Econometrics,* vol. 65, 1995, pp. 9–43.

[9]   Bjurek, H., L. Hjalmarsson, and F.R. Forsund, "Deterministic Parametric and Nonparametric Estimation of Efficiency in Service Production," *Journal of Econometrics,* vol. 46, 1990, pp. 213–227.

[10]  Blackorby, C., and R.R. Russell, "Will the Real Elasticity of Substitution Please Stand Up? (A Comparison of the Allen/Uzawa and Morishima Elasticities)," *American Economic Review,* vol. 79, no. 4, September 1989, pp. 882–888.

[11]  Bodea, Sorin A., "Information Technology and Economic Performance: Is Measuring Productivity Still Useful?," *Program on Information Resources Policy Publication P-94-8,* Center for Information Policy Research, Harvard University, 1994.

[12]  Bozman, J.S., "IS in Healthcare: Shaking off 15 Years of DP-as-Usual," *Computerworld,* January 18, 1988, pp. 61–64.

[13]  Brancheau, J.C., and J.C. Wetherbe, "Key Issues in Information Systems Management," *MIS Quarterly,* vol. 11, no. 1, March 1987, pp. 23–45.

[14]  Breshnahan, T.F., "Measuring the Spillovers from Technical Advance: Mainframe Computers in Financial Services," *American Economic Review,* vol. 76, no. 4, September 1986, pp. 742–755.

[15]  Breyer, F., "The Specification of a Hospital Cost Function: A Comment on the Recent Literature," *Journal of Health Economics,* vol. 6, 1987, pp. 147–158.

[16]  Broom, Cheryle, "Sunset Review of the Washington State Hospital Commission and Related Hospital Cost Containment Issues," *Memo to Legislative Budget Committee,* State of Washington, November 15, 1988.

[17]  Brynjolfsson, E., "The Productivity Paradox of Information Technology," *Communications of the ACM,* vol. 36, No. 12, December 1993, pp. 67–77.

[18]  Brynjolofsson, E., "The Contribution of Information Technology to Consumer Welfare," *Information Systems Research,* vol. 7, no. 3, September 1996, pp. 281–300.

[19]  Brynjolofsson, E., and L.M. Hitt, "Paradox Lost? Firm-Level Evidence on the Returns to Information Systems Spending," *Management Science,* vol. 42, no. 4, April 1996, pp. 541–558.

[20]  Brynjolofsson, E., and S. Yang, "Information Technology and Productivity: A Review of Literature," *Advances in Computers,* vol. 43, 1996, pp. 179–214.

[21]  Bjurek, H., L. Hjalmarsson, and F.R. Forsund, "Deterministic Parametric and Nonparametric Estimation of Efficiency in Service Production: A Comparison," *Journal of Econometrics,* vol. 46, 1990, pp. 213–227.

[22]  Bureau of Labor Statistics, "Trends in Multifactor Productivity," US Department of Labor, Bulletin 2178, September 1983.

[23] Bureau of Statistics, *Statistical Abstracts of the United States,* 1995.

[24] Burgess, J.F., and P.W. Wilson, "Hospital Ownership and Technical Efficiency," *Management Science,* vol. 42, No. 1, January 1996, pp. 110–123.

[25] Carlsson, B., "Productivity Analysis: A Micro-to-Macro Perspective," in *Technology and Investment: Crucial Issues for the 1990s,* E. Deiaco, E. Hornell, and G. Vickery (Eds.), Pinter, London, 1990.

[26] Chambers, R.G., *Applied Production Analysis: A Dual Approach,* Cambridge University Press, 1988.

[27] Charnes, A., W.W. Cooper, and E. Rhodes, "Measuring the Efficiency of Decision Making Units," *European Journal of Operational Research,* vol. 2, no. 6, November 1978, pp. 429–444.

[28] Charnes, A., W.W. Cooper, A.Y. Lewin, and L.M. Seiford, Eds., *Data Envelopment Analysis: The Theory, the Method and the Process,* Kluwer Academic, Boston, 1994.

[29] Chilingerean, J.A., "Evaluating Physician Efficiency in Hospitals: A Multivariate Analysis of Best Practices," *European Journal of Operational Research,* vol. 80, 1995, pp. 548–574.

[30] Christensen, L.R., and W.H. Greene, "Economies of scale in U.S. Electric Power Generation," *Journal of Political Economy,* vol. 84, no. 4, August 1976, pp. 654–676.

[31] Christensen, L.R., and D.W. Jorgenson, "The Measurement of US Real Capital Input, 1929-1967," *The Review of Income and Wealth,* vol. 15, No. 4, 1969, pp. 293–320.

[32] Conrad, D., S. Mick, C. Madden, and C. Hoare, "Vertical Structures and Control in Healthcare Markets: A Conceptual Framework and Empirical Review," *Medical Care Review,* vol. 45, no. 1, 1988, pp. 49–100.

[33] Cowing, T.G., A.G. Holtmann, and S. Powers, "Hospital Cost Analysis: A Survey and Evaluation of Recent Studies," *Advances in Health Economics and Health Services Research,* vol. 4, 1983, pp. 257–303.

[34] David, Paul, "The Dynamo and the Computer: A Historical Perspective on the Modern Productivity Paradox," *American Economic Review,* vol. 80, no. 2, May 1990, pp. 355–361.

[35] David, Paul, "Computer and Dynamo: The Modern Productivity Paradox in a Not-Too-Distant Mirror," in *Technology and Productivity—The Challenge to Economic Policy,* OECD, Paris, 1991.

[36] Debreu, G., "The Coefficient of Resource Utilization", *Econometrica,* vol. 19, no. 3, July 1951, pp. 273–292.

[37] Deiwert, W.E., and T.J. Wales, "Flexible Functional Forms and Global Curvature Conditions," *Econometrica,* vol. 55, 1987, pp. 43–68.

[38]  DeLone, William H., and Ephraim R. McLean, "Information Systems Success: The Quest for the Dependent Variable," *Information Systems Research*, vol. 3, no. 1, March 1992, pp. 60–95.

[39]  Dewan, S., and C. Min, "The Substitution of Information Technology for Other Factors of Production: A Firm-Level Analysis," *Management Science*, Forthcoming, 1997.

[40]  Eakin, B.K., "Allocative Inefficiency in the Production of Hospital Services," *Southern Economic Journal*, vol. 58, no. 1, July 1991, pp. 240–249.

[41]  Eakin, B.K., "Do Physicians Minimize Cost?," in *The Measurement of Productive Efficiency*, H.O. Fried, C.A.K. Lovell and S.S. Schmidt (Eds.), Oxford University Press, 1993, pp. 221–236.

[42]  Eakin, B.K., and T. Kniesner, "Estimating a Non-Minimum Cost Function for Hospitals," *Southern Economic Journal*, vol. 54, no. 3, January 1988, pp. 583–592.

[43]  Eldenburg, L.A., and S. Kallapur, "Changes in Hospital Services Mix and Cost Allocations in Response to Changes in Medicare Reimbursement Scheme," *Journal of Accounting and Economics*, vol. 23, No. 1, May 1997, pp. 31–51.

[44]  Färe, R., S. Grosskopf, and C.A.K. Lovell, *Production Frontiers*, Cambridge University Press, UK, 1994.

[45]  Farrell, M.J., "The Measurement of Productive Efficiency," *Journal of the Royal Statistical Society* Series A, 120, Part 3, pp. 253–281.

[46]  Feldstein, Paul J., *Health Care Economics*, John Wiley and Sons, New York, 1983.

[47]  Flower, J., "Pride and Prejudice," *Healthcare Forum*, vol. 39, no. 2, 1996, pp. 26–34.

[48]  Friedman, B., and Mark V. Pauly, "A New Approach to Hospital Cost Functions and Some Issues in Revenue Regulation," *Healthcare Financing Review*, vol. 4, no. 3, 1983, pp. 105–114.

[49]  Fuchs, Victor R., *The Health Economy*, Harvard University Press, Cambridge, Massachusetts, 1986.

[50]  Fuchs, Victor R., "Economics, Values and Health Care Reform," *American Economic Review*, vol. 86, No. 1, March 1996, pp. 1–24.

[51]  Gong, B.H., and R.C. Sickles, "Finite Sample Evidence on the Performance of Stochastic Frontiers and Data Envelopment Analysis Using Panel Data," *Journal of Econometrics*, vol. 51, 1992, pp. 259–284.

[52]  Greene, William H., *Econometric Analysis*, Prentice-Hall, Englewood Cliffs, New Jersey, 1993.

[53]  Grosskopf, S., D. Margaritis, and V. Valdmanis, "Estimating Output Substitutability of Hospital Services: A Distance Function Approach," *European Journal of Operational Research*, vol. 80, 1995, pp. 575–587.

[54] Hammer, M.J., and J. Champy, *Reengineering the Corporation: A Manifesto for Business Revolution,* Harper Business, 1993.

[55] Harris, J.E., "The Internal Organization of Hospitals: Some Economic Implications," *The Bell Journal of Economics,* 1977, pp. 467–482.

[56] Harris, S.E., and J.L. Katz, "Firm size and the Information Technology Investment Intensity of Life Insurers," *MIS Quarterly,* September 1991.

[57] Health Care Financing Administration, *The New ICD-9-CM Diagnosis-Related Groups Classification Scheme, Grants and Contracts Report,* John Hopkins University Press, Baltimore, 1983.

[58] Henderson, J.C., and J.B. Thomas, "Aligning Business and Information Technology Domains: Strategic Planning in Hospitals," *Hospital and Health Services Administration,* vol. 37, no. 1, Spring 1992, pp. 71–87.

[59] Hern, W., "Information Systems Require a 'Leap of Faith'," *Healthcare Financial Management,* vol. 10, June 1996.

[60] Hitt, L.M., and E. Brynjolofsson, "Productivity, Business Profitability and Consumer Surplus: Three Different Measures of Information Technology Value," *MIS Quarterly,* June 1996, pp. 121–142.

[61] Jenkins, A., "Multiproduct Cost Analysis: Service and Case-type Cost Equations for Ontario Hospitals," *Applied Economics,* vol. 12, March 1980, pp. 103–113.

[62] Johnson, R.L., "The Economic Era of Health Care," *Healthcare Management Review,* Fall 1994, pp. 64–72.

[63] Johnson, R.L., "Hospital Governance in a Competitive Environment," *Healthcare Management Review,* Winter 1995, pp. 75–83.

[64] Jorgenson, D.W., and K. Stiroh, "Computers and Growth," *Computers and Innovation,* vol. 3, 1995, pp. 295–316.

[65] Kelley, Maryellen, "Productivity and Information Technology: The Elusive Connection," *Management Science,* vol. 40, no. 11, November 1994, .pp. 1406–1425.

[66] Kettelhut, M.C., "Strategic Requirements for IS in the Turbulent Healthcare Environment," *Journal of Systems Management,* vol. 43, no. 6, June 1992, pp. 6–9.

[67] Kim, K.K., and J.E. Mitchelman, "An Examination of Factors for the Strategic Use of Information Systems in the Healthcare Industry," *MIS Quarterly,* June 1990, pp. 201–214.

[68] Kimberly, J.R., and M.J. Evanisko, "Organizational Innovation: The Influence of Individual, Organizational and Contextual Factors on Hospital Adoption of Technological and Administrative Innovations," *Academy of Management Journal,* vol. 24, no. 4, December 1981, pp. 689–713.

[69] Koopmans, T.C., "An Analysis of Production as an Efficient Combination of Activities," *Activity Analysis of Production and Allocation,* Cowles Commission for Research in Economics, Monograph 13, Wiley, New York, 1951.

[70] Kumbhakar, S.C., B. Biswas and D. Von Bailey, "A Study of Economic Efficiency of Utah Dairy Farmers: A Systems Approach," *The Review of Economics and Statistics,* 1989, pp. 595–604.

[71] Kumbhakar, S.C., "A Reexamination of Returns to Scale, Density and Technical Progress in US Airlines," *Southern Economic Journal,* vol. 57, no. 2, October 1990, pp. 428–442.

[72] Kumbhakar, S.C., and A. Heshmati, "Technical Change and Total Factor Productivity Growth in Swedish Manufacturing Industries," Working paper, University of Texas at Austin, 1993.

[73] Lawrence, C.M., "The Effect of Ownership Structure and Accounting System Type on Hospital Costs," *Research in Governmental and Nonprofit Accounting,* vol. 6, 1990, pp. 35–60.

[74] Lee, B.T., and A. Barua, "Assessing the Productivity and Impact of Information Technologies in the Manufacturing Sector," Working Paper, University of Arizona, 1996.

[75] Lovell, C.A.K., "Production Frontiers and Production Efficiency," in *The Measurement of Productive Efficiency,* H.O. Fried, C.A.K. Lovell and S.S. Schmidt (Eds.), Oxford University Press, 1993.

[76] Loveman, G.W., "An Assessment of the Productivity Impact of Information Technologies," in *Information Technology and the Corporation of the 1990s,* T.J. Allen and M.S. Scott Morton (Eds.), IT Press, Cambridge, A, 1994.

[77] Mark, J.A., "A BLS Reader on Productivity, Concepts and Measures of Productivity, Bulletin 2171," U.S. Dept of Labor, Bureau of Labor Statistics, Washington, D.C. 1983.

[78] Markus, M.L., and D. Robey, "Information Technology and Organizational Change: Causal Structure in Theory and Research," *Management Science,* vol. 34, no. 5, May 1988, pp. 583–598.

[79] McClellan, M., "Uncertainty, Health-Care Technologies, and Health-Care Choices," *American Economic Review,* vol. 85, no. 2, May 1995, pp. 38–45.

[80] Morrison, E.R., and C.J. Berndt, "High-tech Capital Formation and Economic Performance in US Manufacturing Industries: An Exploratory Analysis," *Journal of Econometrics,* vol. 65, 1995, pp. 9–43.

[81] Newhouse, J.P., "Reimbursing Health Plans and Health Providers: Efficiency in Production versus Selection," *Journal of Economic Literature,* vol. 34, September 1996, pp. 1236–1263.

[82] Oliner, S.D., and D.E. Sichel, "Computers and Output Growth Revisited: How Big Is the Puzzle?," *Brookings Papers on Economic Activity,* vol. 2, 1994, pp. 273–317.

[83] Osterman, P., "New Technology and Work Organization," in *Technology and Investment: Crucial Issues for the 1990s,* E. Deaico, E. Hornell and G. Vickery (Eds.), Pinter, London, 1990.

[84] Palley, M.A., "Hospital Information Systems and DRG Implementation", *Information and Management,* vol. 20, 1990, pp. 227–234.

[85] Palley, M.A., and S. Conger, "Healthcare Information Systems and Formula-Based Reimbursement: An Empirical Study," *Health Care Management Review,* vol. 20, no. 2, 1995, pp. 74–84.

[86] Pauly, M., and M. Redisch, "The Not-For-Profit Hospital as a Physicians' Cooperative," *American Economic Review,* vol. 63, no. 1, March 1973, pp. 87–99.

[87] Posner, R.A., "Theories of Economic Regulation," *The Bell Journal of Economics and Management Sciences,* 1974.

[88] Roach, S.S., "America's Technology Dilemma: A Profile of the Information Economy," *Morgan Stanley Special Economic Study,* New York, 1987.

[89] Roach, S.S., "Services Under Siege: The Restructuring Imperative," *Harvard Business Review,* vol. 39, no. 2, 1991, pp. 82–92.

[90] Romer, P.M., "Crazy Explanations for the Productivity Slowdown," In *NBER Macroeconomics Annual: 1987,* Stanley Fisher (Ed.), MIT Press, Cambridge, 1987.

[91] Rosenberg, C.E., *The Care of Strangers,* The John Hopkins University Press, Baltimore, Maryland, 1987.

[92] Schmidt, P., and C.A.K. Lovell, "Estimating Technical and Allocative Inefficiency Relative to Stochastic Production and Cost Frontiers," *Journal of Econometrics,* vol. 9, 1979, pp. 343–366.

[93] Seiford, L.M., "Data Envelopment Analysis: The Evolution of the State of the Art (1978-1995)," *Journal of Productivity Analysis,* vol. 7, 1996, pp. 99–137.

[94] Seigel, D., and Z. Griliches, "Purchased Services, Outsourcing, Computers, and Productivity in Manufacturing," *Output Measurement in the Service Sectors,* Z. Griliches et al (Eds.), University of Chicago Press, 1992.

[95] Simon, H., "The Steam Engine and the Computer: What Makes Technology Revolutionary?," *EUDCOM Bulletin,* vol. 22, Spring 1986, pp. 2–5.

[96] Skinner, J., "What do Stochastic Frontier Cost Functions Tell Us About Inefficiency?," *Journal of Health Economics,* vol. 13, 1994, pp. 323–328.

[97] Sloan, F.A., M.A. Morrisey, J. Valvona, "Effects of the Medicare Prospective Payment System on Hospital Cost Containment: An Early Appraisal," *The Milbank Quarterly,* vol. 66, no. 2, 1988, pp. 191–220.

[98] Sloan, F.A., M.A. Morrisey, J. Valvona, "Capital Markets and the Growth of Multi-Hospital Systems," *Advances in Health Economics and Health Services Research,* vol. 7, 1992, pp. 83–109.

[99] Soh, C., and M.L. Markus, "How IT Creates Business Value: A Process Theory Synthesis," *Proceedings of the Fifteenth International Conference on Information Systems,* Amsterdam 1995, pp. 29–41.

[100] Stigler, G.J., "The Theory of Economic Regulation," *The Bell Journal of Economics and Management Sciences,* Spring 1971.

[101] Strassman, P.A., *The Business Value of Computers: An Executive's Guide,* Information Economics Press, New Canaan, CT, 1990.

[102] Strassman, P.A., *Information Payoff: The Transformation of Work in the Electronic Age,* Free Press, New York, 1985.

[103] Varian, H.R., *Microeconomic Analysis,* W.W. Norton & Company, 1984.

[104] Varian, H.R., "Goodness-of-Fit in Optimizing Models," *Journal of Econometrics,* vol. 46, 1990, pp. 125–140.

[105] Vitaliano, D.F., "On the Estimation of Hospital Cost Functions," *Journal of Health Economics,* vol. 6, 1987, pp. 305–318.

[106] Vitaliano, D.F. and M. Toren, "Cost and Efficiency in Nursing Homes: A Stochastic Frontier Approach," *Journal of Health Economics,* vol. 13, 1994, pp. 281–300.

[107] WEFA, *U.S. Long-Term Economic Outlook,* Pennsylvania, 1994.

[108] Weill, P., "The Relationship Between Investment in Information Technology and Firm Performance: A Study of the Valve Manufacturing Sector," *Information Systems Research,* vol. 3, no. 4, December 1992, pp. 307–333.

[109] Zimmerman, J., *Accounting for Decision Making and Control,* Irwin 1995.

[110] Zucherman, S., J. Hadley, L. Iezzoni, "Measuring Hospital Efficiency with Frontier Cost Functions," *Journal of Health Economics,* vol. 13, 1994, pp. 255–280.

# Index

Printed in the United States
by Baker & Taylor Publisher Services